ORAL SEX
FOR WOMEN

*Learn the Pleasure Techniques and Positions
Desired by the World's Most Demanding
Women!*

Marisa Rudder

Bestselling Author of Love & Obey and Real Men Worship Women

Available on Amazon Books.

Please contact: Marisa Rudder

Email: femaleledrelationshipbook@gmail.com

Printed in the United States of America Publisher's Cataloging-in-Publication data

ISBN: 978-0-9991804-5-7

Dedication

I would like to dedicate this book to all the strong, brave ladies who have joined or are about to join the Love & Obey movement and the female-led lifestyle. I also dedicate this book to all the men who want to learn how to give women their greatest sexual pleasure – the oral orgasm. Men, through the instruction in this book, you will learn how to fully satisfy your woman's sexual needs. Women have greater sexual desires than you think, and oral sex is necessary to fully satisfy a woman. You must learn to love, obey, and serve your woman's desires. It is also my wish that all men will experience the joy of being a gentleman and living a purpose-driven life of serving a woman in a loving female-led relationship (FLR). If you have not already joined us, please join us now on social media.

You can find out more at our website:
www.loveandobey.com

Or follow me on social media:

FACEBOOK
https://www.facebook.com/femaleledrelationships

TWITTER
https://twitter.com/loveandobeybook

YOUTUBE
https://www.youtube.com/channel/UCkX3wmd934WR103
hStbzbiQ

INSTAGRAM
https://www.instagram.com/femaleledrelationships

Marisa Rudder

WARNING

This book contains adult sexual content. It should not be read by anyone under the age of eighteen years. In addition to sexually explicit and descriptive content, this book contains controversial views supporting goddess worship ideas and practices, as well as a female-led lifestyle. So, please be careful what you ask for in life because you just might get it. Be advised that once you open the door to goddess worship and a female-led lifestyle, there is usually no turning back. Once you've chosen your woman to be your goddess, she will demand a lot from you. This book also discusses and promotes oral sex performed on women in a way that teaches you and your goddess to experience **cosmic orgasms**. These cosmic orgasms can only be achieved through serious goddess worship. For some men, this is very difficult to deal with, while it is a dream come true for others. If you are converting a woman in your life from plain Jane to goddess, make sure that you are ready and willing to live a female-led lifestyle before inviting her into it. If you are looking for a goddess to worship in your life, ensure that you have made a firm decision to serve her and you have a strong desire to live this female-led lifestyle before building a relationship with a dominant *Love & Obey* goddess.

Introduction

L ove & Obey women in female-led relationships are some of the most ambitious, dynamic, inspiring women you will ever meet, but they are demanding. They require to be in charge, leading in all aspects of their lives. The Love & Obey movement encompasses female empowerment, feminism, and female-led marriages where women lead as the queen and men serve by being supportive gentlemen. Let's face it, when you allow your woman, who enjoys being in power, to be the supreme leader and you raise her up to be the magnificent goddess she can be, you change your life. Part of keeping your queen completely satisfied, happy, and in a great mood every single day is satisfying her with great oral sex. Boring sex creates boring relationships, which don't last long. One of the reasons sex tends to get boring very fast is because women are unsatisfied and sexual activities become as lame as doing chores – cleaning the dishes, taking out the garbage, and mowing the lawn. You run into your room or roll over in the morning, and in five minutes it's done when you orgasm. You roll over, she looks happy, and everyone gets on with their day. But guess what ? She's not happy. Studies show that 25 percent to 74 percent of women have faked an orgasm, so chances are your queen has as well. But think of how life would be if you could actually be certain you gave your queen a mind-blowing orgasm every day. Well now you can. This book is going to teach you everything you need to know about how to fully satisfy your woman by placing her pleasure first. You will be making it your mission, if you choose to accept it, to make her orgasm the focus of your sex. You will become a pro at giving her the best oral sex she has ever had, and this is going to keep her coming back for more.

Not only is this going to change the dynamics of your relationship, but you are going to reap the rewards of a happy wife, happy life. Oral sex is also crucial to your queen's well-being and her health. You might be surprised by how much you enjoy it, not to mention the attention you get in return. You may have tried all the sex positions and role play, but at the end of the day, you are giving your goddess the gift that she can't and her vibrator can't give her – mind-blowing oral sex. A significant part of finding and keeping a female-led woman is that a man must show his complete service to her. Part of this service is being a great lover. Why has Casanova been remembered for centuries? Not because he was great at his job or he could fix cars. If you're going to keep your woman happy, you will need to master the bedroom, and that means becoming a pro at fully satisfying your woman with oral sex.

Oral sex has been around for centuries. It's been called by so many names – cunnilingus, or perhaps slang terms like going down, going downtown, eating her out, pussy licking, sucking clam or sucking oysters, munching carpet, or perhaps some other equally ridiculous slang term commonly used to describe it. Although there are a variety of slang terms people use to describe giving oral sex pleasure to a woman, in this book we are going to call it with the proper respect it deserves – female-led oral sex. The reason I put the emphasis on *female-led* is because you are giving your queen the ultimate sexual experience, one in which she is the focus at all times. Men have given oral sex previously, but going down on your woman for a few minutes while you get all excited to penetrate her is not female-led oral sex. When you are in a female-led relationship, it is mandatory that the sex be for her pleasure. So not only are you going to give her the best sexual experience she's ever had, but you are going to approach the entire sexual act as service to her. Oral sex, to a woman, is the most important skill you will need to master if you want to call yourself a great lover. It is necessary to keep her sexually satisfied. Today there are many variations of female-led relationships, some where women are choosing to cuckold a man and get a better lover. This won't be necessary when you learn to satisfy her fully in ways she has never experienced before. In fact, your woman will probably orgasm more from oral sex than when having intercourse alone, and this is a win-win situation for both of you. Part of oral sex is understanding how it relates to goddess worship and reaching the divine. In the beginning, I will explain a bit about this before moving on to more instruction about performing oral sex. It is important that you understand the context in which you are having sex in a female-led relationship. Performing oral sex on a woman is a powerful and serious lovemaking technique that is not to be taken lightly. Done properly it will change your sex life and more importantly your woman's sex life. Ultimately, it can make you and your woman have a great love life together, and sharing love between people is what it is all about in life.

Oral sex should never be faked, played, or simulated. If you don't want to give her oral sex, it's the same as her not wanting to have intercourse with you. You may orgasm easily during sex, but most women don't. In addition, if she's not enjoying oral sex because your technique is off or you don't know what you are doing, this can be the beginning of disaster. Unhappy wife, disastrous life. Today, it is important for men to learn how to master oral sex if they're going to keep a strong, demanding queen in a female-led relationship happy. Bad oral sex makes a woman feel uncomfortable and makes you seem unsure of yourself. Don't do as the comedian Sam Kinison instructs. He said, "You perform oral sex on a woman by writing out the letters of the alphabet with your tongue on a woman's clitoris." This gets you in the doghouse really fast and leaves you with a raging, unhappy, unsatisfied woman.

Yes, I will teach you the tried-and-true technical moves to bring a woman to orgasm during oral sex, but this is nothing compared to what you can learn if you choose to read this book carefully and learn how to truly bow before a goddess and make love to her with your mouth and tongue. I will show you how to achieve a mind-bowing orgasm I call the *cosmic orgasm*. It is so powerful, you will feel like you are having an orgasm with her as she comes in your mouth. The Divine Oral Sex I am describing can result in true joy and spiritual orgasm that will heal your soul and make you feel like the king of the world. It will be the greatest enhancement of your love life within your present relationship and will unlock a new level of passion between you and your woman.

The success of oral sex and creating true pleasure while practicing oral sex for your goddess, as well as your own joy of practicing oral sex, depends on one thing and one thing alone: your mental state of mind must be sincere and dedicated to bringing pleasure to your woman. Do you truly want to love, obey, and serve a woman? The truly loving, obedient, and service-oriented man is the one who will always really enjoy giving oral sex. Oral sex practiced with this mental focus on love, obedience, and service as your style of making love will always lead to an easy and fast orgasm for your woman.

Fake oral sex is the worst oral sex! Oral sex practiced without a mental focus on true love, obedience, and service to a woman will be performed without true pleasure for the man practicing it. This fake oral sex performance will only lead to no oral sex orgasm, difficulties in experiencing orgasm from oral sex, or a very delayed orgasm from oral sex! An orgasm may be achieved, but it will be nothing compared to the real thing, and it definitely will not be a life-changing *cosmic orgasm.*

To become an artist and deliver divine bliss to your woman, you must be genuinely devoted to loving, obeying, and serving her and putting her pleasure first. The power of love will give you the strength, purity of heart, and connection to the feminine divine to dissolve anything and all that might still be separating you at this very moment from achieving the ultimate cosmic orgasm with your goddess. So take a look inside, gentleman, observe your very own present attitude and feelings toward your present female partner, and make proper adjustments and give total freedom to your partner.

Make a decision: Do you want to commit and make your partner fully happy, right now? Do you want to make a genuine effort to achieve love, to be obedient to her, and to serve all her needs and bring her pleasure, or not? Do you want you and your partner to find true love and absolute long-lasting bliss and happiness in your relationship, or not? I'm not saying you can't have sex with a stranger or a casual acquaintance, you can. However, you will not experience what we are going for in this book.

You simply may be searching for a replacement or are uninterested in this real Divine art of providing breathtaking oral sex to a goddess, and you may only want acceptance as a good lover who technically knows what to do and how to move his tongue back and forth until she orgasms. I'm not here to judge you. Everyone is at a different stage in their evolution of their lovemaking skills and their relationships. If this is what you want, don't be disappointed; you will still learn the technical skills you need to be a good lover and a skilled provider of oral sex in this book. But if you want more, if you want to discover the truly divine sexual being – "the Divine Cosmic Force of the Universe" – you can find that in this book as well. Maybe your main focus right now is searching for a great career, getting into a better social position, making more money, driving a fancier car, living in a bigger home, or getting more degrees and diplomas. Maybe you are looking for happiness in anything material, but these superficial social goals are a weak substitute for true love and the ultimate loving acceptance of yourself and your partner as beautiful, simple, spiritual, and sexual beings, expressing your divine connection with the universe through your physical bodies in this lifetime. Your mind is the most powerful sex organ in your body, and you will be missing such powerful, mind-blowing true love in all of its amazing manifestations, like divine oral sex, if you're in the wrong state of mind – and you will simply end up looking for more and more material substitutes in this world for what you really want – *true love*!

Yes, we all know that there are many things money can buy – even oral sex from a prostitute. But nothing can buy or even temporarily replace truly divine, sweet love between truly loving and spiritually connected partners. Only your true love for another person and their true love back to you can free your true love and give you the ultimate connection and the resulting *cosmic orgasms*. So read about the beauty of a female-led relationship and how devoting your life to women can free your soul and make you happier than you ever imagined possible. And don't worry, right after this we will get into the hardcore instructions on how to give great oral sex, even without being in love.

Table of Contents

Marisa Rudder

CHAPTER 1

A Love & Obey female-led relationship gives you an opportunity to serve your goddess as a supportive gentleman. Part of finally getting into a proper female-led lifestyle is to completely submit and allow your woman to be in charge. Women lead, period, and men follow in all aspects of the relationship. This means that she is also in charge in the bedroom. Sex is an important part of any relationship and even more important in the female-led relationship because men no longer dominate the bedroom, but now they have a new role. They serve women by making the sexual experience all about her, and in doing so, they must give her the best oral sex she's ever had.

In female-led relationships, men must put aside the male ego to be really successful, where the ultimate goal is to love, obey, and serve the female. In the bedroom this is extremely important because it is the one place where both men and women come together to build intimacy. Sex can be viewed as the key to opening up channels of better connection, better attachment, and better intimacy with your partner as is discussed in *Psychology Today.* In a Love & Obey female-led relationship, the woman is a goddess, and the man devotes his life to worshipping her in and out of the bedroom. Sex becomes an act of worship, and it becomes focused on the woman's pleasure because this now becomes the way you will connect to her each and every day. I believe it is the strong cosmic connection that happens during oral sex that bonds two people so intimately.

You learn that your pleasure only comes from how much pleasure you can give your woman. Sexually, your focus is on your goddess's orgasms and all of her desires being fulfilled. Oral sex offers an opportunity for you to connect to her Feminine Divine —Mother Universe, the source of all life. By learning the Love & Obey methods of oral sex, you will not only be giving your queen the best sex she has ever had, but also your complete devotion by connecting to her on a physical, mental, and now spiritual level.

This book will give you the tools you need to be a great lover and be a great servant to your goddess. It will change the way you approach your relationship daily, because by fully satisfying your queen, you place her on a pedestal and become her support system so she can feel empowered and confident to do her job as leader of your lives and your relationship. Women are changed when they are in a female-led relationship. They feel happy, inspired, and loved each and every day, and you feel accepted, valuable, and special in return because you have created this change in her. There is nothing like a powerful woman who is free to be the queen.

Before we get into the actual techniques on how to give her mind-blowing orgasms through oral sex, I will explain more about how oral sex creates the pathway to unleash the divine energy. Then I will cover everything you need to know about the vagina and how to bring it to climax. You will become master of the bedroom with each and every session. Through oral pleasure you release her inner goddess and you connect to it. This connection will form a powerful bond between you and your queen. Love & Obey oral sex proves true and full acceptance of your female partner as your divine goddess and female leader who rules your life. By going into service of her in the bedroom, you are performing a ritual to connect to her inner divine. This is only achieved by the mastery of performing oral sex and giving her the best climax she can achieve.

Today millions of women rule over their husbands in female-led relationships, whether it is as the primary financial provider or the man is the provider allowing her to be the queen. Female-led relationships are becoming more common with celebrities, athletes, and executives, and they have always been alive and well with the wealthy class. Why ? because strong powerful men know the value of a strong queen. How much stronger is the kingdom than when there is a strong, powerful queen with an equally strong king placing her on a pedestal and allowing her to take charge. This is the basis of a female-led relationship. The man is not weak or insignificant. He is the general, the supporting force in the relationship. Women are no longer riding in the passenger seat; they are the drivers. I know many real-life examples of where women taking charge of their lives, careers, and relationships resulted in dramatically changing their men's lives. There are so many prominent examples – British royalty, the queen is in charge; female prime ministers, female entrepreneurs running corporations, female athletes like Serena Williams and Julie Ertz, even celebrities like Jennifer Lopez. All examples of strong women leading in their fields with their men supporting them. Such powerful women are too strong today and better lovers, and men need to learn to be submissive partners. Men will attract love by being obedient gentlemen and hoping to attract great women as a result of recognizing the female's natural loving authority over them. Men must attract women now by offering true love, obedience, and service that requires them to give everything to satisfy the desires and needs of the superior female. Women now will have men for the heavy housework and home repair, as well as convenient providers of sexual satisfaction.

In patriarchal times, the only person who could control a man was a woman. There are so many examples of how powerful men were brought to their knees, good or bad, by women. Wallace Simpson changed the course of history when King Edward abdicated the throne. King Henry VIII, notorious womanizer, made his mistress Anne Boleyn a queen and went against the church to do it, for a woman. There are even modern-day examples, like Bill Clinton's impeachment because of a woman, and Prince Harry marrying a bi-racial common American woman and now moving away from the monarchy to live their own lives in North America – all under a woman's influence. Women are powerful in many areas, so in the female-led relationship, you are submitting to that power. You show your ultimate respect in the bedroom, which was once an area of male dominance, and now becomes a place of worship of the female.

So why does this work so effortlessly? Women have become accustomed to taking charge. In *Gone with the Wind* I was always so fascinated by when the men went off to war and the women still continued to survive and took charge. In a world when women were always expected to follow men, in their absence, they stepped up and managed everything. Women have a natural ability to lead because they are multi-taskers and great communicators. Women form relationships with other people better than men. They are collaborators, and nothing can get done as an island. Today in 2020, women are finally exercising their natural ability to be the ruler, and men can be all they can be as the supporter. Oral sex is part of the supportive duties. Sex becomes your ultimate chance to show your Goddess how much you adore her. Your willingness to ensure her happiness will transform your life's purpose. When men discover their "New Life Purpose" of loving, obeying, and serving a superior female, they will find peace and contentment. In addition, the loving female authority who rules over him will provide him with tremendous amounts of love and affection.

I do not recommend cruel abuse like a traditional dominatrix. I believe that abuse is not love and does not build a long-term relationship. Often such fem dom marriages are accompanied by out-of-the-ordinary marriage contracts which cause men to feel conflicted, weak, and powerless. No organism ever wants to feel powerless. Even ants that work for the queen being busy building the fortress don't feel weak. They know their purpose, and they go about it daily. They are empowered to serve the queen. Beating men, locking them up in animal cages, and having them wear female lingerie may be activities that some couples choose to engage in, but this is not the basis for building a successful female-led relationship, which is built on the strength of both partners, not weakness.

In a female-led relationship, women rule and men obey. Men must have respect for a woman's power and authority. The more you spiritually accept her Feminine Divine and her goddess powers, the more you understand the importance of giving her a great sexual experience.

CHAPTER 2

The female-led relationship offers an opportunity to explore more than just a great daily life with your queen. It gives you a chance to improve all aspects of her life, making her a greater leader and a more confident woman and connecting to her on the deepest level possible. Oral sex is the pathway to the divine. The vagina and uterus give life, and many believe that it is a connection to the spiritual realm. Why is this important? Humans are not just physical creatures. We are mental, physical, and spiritual beings, and many times unhappiness in individuals and relationships can stem from the inability to satisfy all parts. As the man in your queen's life, you learned that it was your duty to ensure that your woman feels fully served. In daily life this is accomplished by doing everything she commands and allowing her to take control in all aspects of your life. Sex is an extremely important part of your service, and now you will be able to connect to her on levels that no one else can. In the bedroom, you will now be charged with giving your queen the ultimate sexual experience by making the sex all about her and placing the focus on her. By doing this, you will gain great pleasure as well, because you will not only feel more satisfied in your own orgasms but you will be confident that you are solely responsible for giving her the ultimate sexual pleasure.

Oral sex becomes the center of the entire sexual session because oral sex is the main method most women require to climax effectively. Now you become the most important person in her life. One of the exciting parts of a female-led relationship is sharing as many new experiences in your daily life as possible. Now, as a man, you are supporting your woman on her path to connecting to the Feminine Divine, the Divine Cosmic Force of the Universe. This divine connection will enhance your present relationship and bring a new energy into your life. Tantric masters have long preached the importance of sexual energy. This is so powerful they use it to transcend. They learn techniques to expand and deepen the orgasm experience. In female-led oral sex, this is what you are doing for your goddess. Sex becomes the ritual you will perform throughout the entire session to help your goddess have that mind-blowing cosmic experience together with her orgasm. Your sex becomes a ceremony, a celebration of the divine. You become more connected to the universe when you bring your goddess to orgasm, and you too are experiencing the euphoria. In tantric sex, the male energy is like fire – burning hot and fast, but a woman's energy is like water, it flows. It is this difference that makes female-led oral sex so much more complex. You will no longer think of your male ego or your male pleasure. You will no longer receive oral sex or a blow job unless your goddess desires it for her own reasons. You will now live to bring pleasure to your goddess first. Once her needs are fulfilled, then you can fulfill yours. The difference with focusing on her pleasure is that it takes a very precise technique to be able to get her sufficiently aroused and to ensure she is satisfied. The entire sex session is done with her at the center. I raise the example of Henry VIII. Only Anne Boleyn, who made Henry wait to have sex until they were married and controlled his every mood, received his undivided attention during sex. Henry had thousands of lovers that he just fucked and left, but Anne forced him to learn to seduce her and place her above even his closest advisors. This was a revolution at the time, since the opinion of a woman even at royal levels was never considered. Women were virtually invisible. But Anne Boleyn was one of the first women at that time to essentially create a female-led relationship with someone who was, at the time, the most powerful man on the planet.

That is the power of female-led. Once you fully commit to satisfying your goddess, you will receive a tremendous energy boost and strengthening of your worship of your queen. I recommend performing oral sex on your woman as often as she will allow. Personally, I demand daily oral worship and praise of me as the goddess. I see it as very crucial to my overall well-being. Oral sex changes a woman's eagerness for sex because she knows it's for her pleasure. How can you resist someone who wants to worship you? I feel that one of the greatest ways to show your devotion is to serve your woman's every desire, and this includes every sexual desire. It is important that you make her feel truly adored and worshipped during sex. You must allow her the time to relax and forget about all of the stresses of life. This is her moment of fantasy and adventure. Take her to another place with sex that fulfills her to the core.

Connecting to your goddess's divine through the vagina helps to strengthen the relationship among many other health benefits. First, when you make sex about lovemaking and worship, orgasms are much easier to achieve and they raise oxytocin which helps to combat stress and regulate cortisol in the body. People sleep better, regulate appetite and hormones, and report feeling happy and positive. So when you focus on your goddess's pleasure, you are improving all facets of her being. You are ensuring that all aspects of her life are fulfilled. Connecting to the divine through sex improves your spiritual connection, which is the most powerful way to be connected. I feel that today, this is the missing link. People have become very dissatisfied with religions and many belief systems, and I believe that this is because we were constantly looking for pastors, priests, or churches to create happiness in our lives. The spiritual connection to the universe, divine, and God lies within us, so as partners in a union the responsibility is on you and your queen to create the happiness you are seeking through the daily activities in your relationship. This is what makes female-led so special. The feminine represents mother earth. This is one of the greatest powers in the universe. When you unleash this power in your goddess, you open up pathways to improve your lives exponentially because both male and female energy are released. Einstein said, "Energy can neither be created nor destroyed." This means that energy is a real and powerful force, ever present. There are some practitioners who believe that we can manifest through the use of sexual energy. This is part of Tantra teachings, and it is believed that through the harnessing of sexual energy, it is possible to achieve enlightenment. But traditional intercourse where the focus is on the man is much more about releasing energy than building it and harnessing. This can only happen through the worship of the woman through oral sex and in so doing prolonging the experience, which then takes both people to higher levels. It is my belief that several groups knew the power of Tantra and sexual energy and made it their mission to destroy and try to bury it. The Crusaders destroyed much of the Tantra teachings. But today, there are many sex goddesses who swear by the power of sexual energy. If sexual energy can create life, it can help to manifest great things in your life. I believe that it is the breakdown and lack of sexual connection with the focus of connecting to the feminine divine that is the source of the overall breakdown of the relationship. As the main supporter and servant to your queen, the responsibility falls on your shoulders. You will need to create the right experience in which you will use and harness the sexual energy you create with your queen to enrich the relationship. Why is it the man's responsibility? By nature, men are much more aggressive about sex. So instead of focusing that sexual aggression on a sex act which lasts a few minutes and largely leaves the goddess unsatisfied, you can now create a sexual experience for your goddess which fulfills her on a physical, mental, and spiritual level and leaves her wanting more. You can only achieve this by making her the center of your lovemaking center by becoming a master of oral sex. Oral sex is not new. Explicit illustrations on pottery date back as early as 300 BC, and similar graphic depictions of cunnilingus dating from 200 BC appear on scrolls from China and Japan. Even the most famous love manual of them all, the Kama Sutra, written by Indian author and philosopher Vatsyayana in 400 AD, places emphasis on "oral congress" with women. Kissing the yoni is praised in India, and interestingly he says it is a much more important practice for great sex than oral sex performed on a man. This is an ancient female-led statement of truth. Through the centuries erotic art has contained many references to oral sex performed on women, such as the explicit carvings of "yoni kisses" found in twelfth-century Indian temples.

In addition, to the spiritual effects of sex, there are so many favorable health effects which come from weekly sex sessions. Research shows that women who are having great sexual experiences weekly are less likely go into menopause. Less sex has been linked to early menopause. *Science Daily* reported that USA's "Study of Women's Health Across the Nation," the largest, most diverse, and most representative longitudinal cohort study available to research aspects of the menopause transition, found that if a woman is not having sex and there is no chance of pregnancy, then the body "chooses" not to invest in ovulation, as it would be pointless. There may be a biological energetic trade-off between investing energy into ovulation and investing elsewhere, like raising grandchildren. This means that women will be less interested in sex as they go into menopause, which screams disaster for a relationship. But this is great news as now, you and your queen can prolong your sex life well into later life. Many relationships begin to break down when people are in their fifties and sixties, so keeping a strong sexual connection as you age becomes of great importance to the strength of the relationship. The great thing about oral sex is, the more you practice, the better you get. So there is no limit to how great you can be at sexually satisfying your queen. Many couples get into trouble if as the man ages he develops erectile dysfunction or sexual performance is affected by conditions or use of medications. If the focus is on the woman's pleasure, this becomes a less serious issue.

CHAPTER 3

O ne of the reasons oral sex has been so downplayed during most sexual sessions is the lack of understanding of the vagina by men and women. Unlike the penis, which is outside the body, much of the workings of the vagina is on the inside. Women can't even see their vagina without contorting into a strange position, trying to use a well-placed mirror. Hence, most women and men have never actually seen the vagina. I was once horrified to learn how many women never allow a man to see them fully nude in the light or covered up under blankets. In a female-led relationship, a woman's entire body including her vagina must be worshiped by men. You will need to learn how to get your goddess so relaxed that she willingly allows you to explore her body and learn everything you can about her vagina.

Becoming a master of oral sex will be how you demonstrate your ultimate devotion to her. I hope that even for couples who are in open relationships, you reserve oral sex for the special bonding with your queen. Oral sex must be enacted like a ceremony. One of the big things missing in sex lives is the idea of ceremony. Lingerie, candles, satin sheets are all part of the ceremony. I once had a conversation with a friend.

It was Valentine's Eve, and I asked her what she was preparing and wearing for her husband for Valentine's night. I asked, "What kind of lingerie will you wear?" She replied, "None." She had never owned lingerie and had been married for over twenty years. I was shocked and promptly suggested she go get something super sexy for the night. Female-led women generally know that the ceremony of sex is very important and it's the little things that add up to a fantastic experience. So as the queen's servant and the man, you will need to prepare for the ceremony of oral sex. Get a nice big pillow you reserve only for sex, get a fun wedge to put her hips up on, candles, massage oils – anything you can to make the space special. Buy her sexy underwear that you'll want to feel before you begin and see her walking around in. You need to partake in making sex a special experience. Reading this book is a great start because you will be able to delight her when you can show off your oral skills. Don't feel bad if you have all these questions in your head: "Does my woman's vagina look like a mystery down there?" "What the heck do I do?" "Where do I begin?" "What's the best area to focus on?" It can be confusing. There are inner and outer flaps and folds of skin and maybe some hair, then even more folds and more flaps, and then the flower, the bud of the clitoris. "Do I lick, kiss; rough, soft, teasing?" You will have a million questions, and I will do my best to answer all. But remember this one guiding principle – it all works, and you need to gauge how your queen is turned on by it. You need to become very tuned into how she is feeling. I am amazed at how many couples never discuss sex. After a sex session, it is mandatory to ask what worked, what she liked and did not like. During sex, it is fun to ask, "You like that?" "how does that feel?" These are the conversations to have, not just random, "Ooh, babe, I like that," or "Hit it hard." The worst is when men feel the need to talk all the way through. There is a time and place. Oral sex is a time when your woman wants to be relaxed and you are modifying your technique to learn what works for her. It's not a session you are trying to get through so you can get to intercourse. You will approach oral sex like it's the main course, not the appetizer. We savor the main course in a meal like it's the best food we have ever had, and this is the approach you take when performing oral sex.

One of the most important things to do with sex is to get your goddess in the mood. Too many men underestimate the importance of this. If your queen is stressed from the day, the first thing you want to do is get her to relax. This is the lead-up. Take over the chores – cooking diner, doing the dishes, or other chores. Surprise her by drawing her a nice bath or giving her a massage. Let her unwind by discussing anything she wants to talk about. When she is relaxed, she is more likely to entertain having sex. I think surprises are a great way to show a woman you really care and you are really interested in fulfilling her needs. In the past, I cannot really recall one time when my partners, even in long-term relationships, brought me flowers or some other gift for no reason. I cannot recall one time my bath was drawn or anything was done just because. Today, this happens almost every day, without me ever having to mention it. So when you are trying to seduce your goddess, do the unexpected. You being excited about oral sex should delight her.

When you are finally in bed ready to have sex, begin slowly and gently. Make sure she is in a comfortable position. Tell her you are going to be switching it up if you have not had oral sex for a long time. Get her in the mood first. I cannot stress the importance of this. Kiss her neck, her lips, her breasts, her chest, and her navel, making your way down. Savor each moment as though you are discovering her body for the first time. Tell her how beautiful she is, how much you love the feel of her curves and her skin. It's going to be so much more soothing when you keep the focus on your queen at all times.

Men often underestimate the power of a compliment. Now you are going to be performing oral sex like there is a real art to it.

While you are performing oral sex, you may have a lot of thoughts going through your mind. You may wonder, "Is she enjoying it?" "Am I doing this correctly?" Be confident, look for clues. Is she relaxed? Is she moaning? Is she smiling? If she isn't, ask questions: "How is this?" "Do you like this?" In the beginning, it should be much more like you are teasing her. You're getting her excited. You're kissing outside her panties, then slowly slipping them off. Maintaining eye contact. Every movement and eye contact should be deliberate. You're watching her breathing, her noises, the look on her face. You are maintaining all the focus on her enjoyment. The idea is to slowly seduce her as you are getting her excited.

Now you are ready to give mind-blowing oral sex to your queen. Your focus should always be on how you can connect to the divine force and energy in her, how you can get her to come alive. One of the worst experiences I discussed with a man was about his wife, who was a gorgeous model, but she lay on the bed, making no sound or movement while he was performing any sex act. I saw this as a huge problem, and I suggested that he needed to have a talk with her. You need to have open communication and feedback from your goddess. If you cannot determine if she enjoys the sex or how she feels, you will need to request feedback directly. It's the only way you will learn and improve your skills.

Every Love & Obey female-led woman loves oral sex and enjoys it again and again. In fact, there are very few women on the planet who don't grow to absolutely enjoy oral sex done right. You are now challenged to become a master of giving it. You will be rewarded with a happy partner who will be so much more enthusiastic about sex. If you are single and in the dating world, learning how to dominate a woman in the bedroom with killer oral skills moves you up the ranks quickly. You may find that you connect with your ideal woman much faster because your connection is so much deeper. Women will flock to you in the dating world because it's very difficult to find men who are enthusiastic. When men are able to fully satisfy a goddess, relationships can be turned around. I have successfully saved many relationships from failure and marriages from divorce with the simple concepts in all of my female-led books, and I know that when a man masters oral sex, it changes the focus in the bedroom, and it can change the course of a relationship. My name isn't Rudder for nothing. A rudder steers the ship in the right direction. A relationship is still a ship which need to be steered, and that's what I do. Men are always asking what they should do when their goddess is resistant to oral sex. Here is a secret: there are many reasons why women say they don't like oral sex, and it usually comes down to two reasons: (1) they are brainwashed by the archaic rules that the man needs to be satisfied first, or (2) they have never had anyone who was good at it and enthusiastic about it. I often listen to the lyrics in rap music, and rarely do I ever hear a male rapper talking about getting down and licking pussy. But I hear it more from the females, and today women are insisting on it. So in the words of a famous female musician, "You gotta lick it, before you kick it."

CHAPTER 4

T he spiritual aspects of oral sex have proved to be important, but how to perform oral sex is even more important to achieve the goal of total goddess satisfaction. It's time for you to get started. Sex therapist Megan Fleming says that "all arousal begins with relaxation." How you achieve this for your woman is important. Are you supporting her in chores and household duties? Have you placed her on a pedestal calling her your queen or goddess? Are you light, positive, and enthusiastic? Women are going to be much more in the mood if they don't have to come home to more stressors. It's important to begin to put your woman in the mood early in the day. Send her a text saying how much you love her and how much she turns you on. Send flowers for no reason. Meet her for a drink after work. I have spoken with hundreds of couples in a female-led relationship, and many of the women admit that it is the actions of their men which really help put them in the mood. Even though your woman is in charge, you are still committed to getting her relaxed, happy, and turned on to have mind-blowing sex. One ritual which must be avoided is sitting on the couch. On the night you are getting ready to worship your queen, do anything you can to avoid sitting on the sofa watching TV. You want to draw her a bath, lay out her favorite lingerie, set the mood, and wait in the bedroom with candles, massage oil, and sex toys. She must be instructed to come to bed early so you can begin with a nice long massage and caressing. Do not eat a heavy dinner, so both of you can feel comfortable. Set the mood by beginning with touching her hair, kissing and massaging. Play her favorite music, use candles and sweet scents, and do everything with care. Remove all distractions – phones, laptops, and pets, and put the kids to bed.

The setup is vitally important. You may be tempted just to go into robot mode and end up moving to intercourse as fast as you can. In my experience many men don't enjoy licking a vagina because they feel insecure in doing it. They lead by thinking of all the reasons they hate it. This attitude has to change. Look at it as a challenge. You're going to master the art of oral sex, one step at a time. Give yourself permission to spend a short time just thinking about your goddess. Forget 100 percent about your own needs and begin this way. Communicate with your goddess. How does she want oral sex performed? Let her decide. I will offer a number of effective positions in later chapters that you can use to keep it exciting. The important thing is you show that you are serious about serving her needs first.

Sometimes a warm bath with candles and some wine can help get her in the mood. You will need to set this up for her. Make it a sweet surprise. Date night is another way to get in the mood. Get outside the house to have some fun before returning home to serve your queen. Keep it interesting. Change it up. No one likes the same boring routine each week, and boredom is the kiss of death for relationships. It will not be necessary to know exactly what to do right away. Women don't expect you to know exactly how they want their pussy licked or caressed. She is willing to talk you through what she likes. And when she does, take time to listen intently. Receive her information as a gift. Cherish some new personal knowledge about her. You may not like being told what to do, but you will become a much better lover if you listen to what she wants.

Let's review some important fundamentals. Some women initially may say they don't feel comfortable receiving oral sex. For some women, this is due to insecurities about their scent or taste, or their internalized beliefs that their pussy is "ugly." Some worry that men find the experience unpleasant. Others dislike being the center of attention or find themselves unable to relax when everything is focused on their pleasure. In our society, women (except for maybe Victoria's Secret models) feel hypercritical about their bodies, so having your eyes, nose, and mouth right in the middle of one of the most private and intimate part of a woman's body is going to evoke some insecurity and at least a little resistance. Many women are already self-conscious about their weight, how their body looks, whether they have a small, flat butt or too much fat on their legs or stomach. So you will have to learn how to handle your queen's insecurities. This is an area that men do not excel in, so it will take some guidance and patience. You will need to be understanding and try to be complimentary and not critical, no matter what she says. The importance of making her feel accepted and loved cannot be overemphasized. During oral sex, your queen wants to open herself to you, and the more relaxed and empathetic you are to her, the more she will be able to let go and enjoy the experience.

You're not going to be able to completely change a woman's perception of her body in one fell tongue swoop, but you can make a special effort to help her feel loved. If you don't love performing oral sex on a woman, never let it be known. In a female-led relationship, you will need to change your attitude toward it. Oral sex for her is not to be viewed as "foreplay." It is the main event, and you need to make her feel excited and enthusiastic about it.

Re-enforce that giving oral sex turns you on and you are hell-bent on making her love every second of it. Some couples will want to add watching porn movies to get in the mood. This is acceptable as long as it's what she wants. My suggestion is not to spend too long, just long enough to get you both in the mood. I cannot stress re-enforcement enough. Tell her that her scent is provocative and it turns you on. Once you get down there, stop for a moment and tell her that you love the way she tastes. Tell her her pussy is fantastic, it's powerful and you love everything about it. If you can convey each of these beliefs to her in a sincere way, you're going to be on your way to giving head and getting ahead. Once you get down there, taking your time is another great way to help her feel more relaxed and excited about what you have in store for her. Begin slowly. Caress, massage, kiss, and draw out the initial contact. This is the foreplay. You want to ensure she is really in the mood. Too many men cut this short and get down to the vagina too fast. Women will never enjoy oral sex if the foreplay is rushed. Many times, this is the problem with intercourse. The foreplay is rushed, and she doesn't have time to relax then its wham bam, thank you, ma'am. This is forbidden in oral sex. You need to give her time to build her divine energy, and you almost need to be going into your own state of euphoria as you get down to performing your mind-blowing oral sex on her.

After complimenting her, start to move slowly down her stomach and thigh. Take your time kissing, hugging, touching, and even talking a little bit more about how going down on her has been a fantasy of yours and you're really excited. Make sure she's aroused before you dive in between her legs. Once you're down there, continue taking your time and start with light licks from the bottom of her pussy to the top. The clitoris is extremely sensitive, so you don't want to dive in right away. The reason why oral sex is so powerful is the clitoris. It is the main region of focus of oral sex for her, but you want to take your time getting there. The clitoris is the most nerve-rich part of a woman's body. The clitoral glans contains about eight thousand nerve endings, making it the powerhouse of pleasure. To get some perspective, that's twice as many nerve endings as the penis. And its potential doesn't end there. This tiny erogenous zone spreads to fifteen thousand other nerves in the vagina area, which explains why women love oral sex so much. We know women are all unique, and the pussy is not any different, so every woman's pussy and even their clits are different. Every woman needs a different kind of stimulation to feel satisfied, depending on her unique biology. For some women, it's so sensitive that she may not want it to be stimulated directly. Some women may prefer touching near and around the clitoris but not directly on it because it is simply too sensitive with direct stimulation. Other women are fine with direct stimulation and even want you to suck on it until they orgasm. Oh, and one more thing, we've all heard about the infamous G-spot. Maybe you've been confused about where it is or how to find it. This notorious pleasure zone became sensationalized back in the eighties when it was believed that if you could only access the G-spot inside the vagina, it would promote female orgasm. But now we know that some women have more sensitivity from the internal parts of the clitoral complex. That's why some women prefer vaginal penetration and intercourse more than other women. It may take a bit of time for you to learn how to stimulate all the right areas, but with practice comes perfection, which is why it is important to have regular sex and to engage in oral sex with your goddess as the focus. Anyone can slip the penis in and move back and forth until you orgasm. It takes a real Casanova to master giving great oral sex to your queen.

There is also the opportunity to add sex toys. These can add lots of variation and excitement. The following are the best sex toys available for her. Vibrators are probably the most common type of sex toy. Wand vibrators are more intense with higher RPM. They can also be great massagers for shoulders, legs, and back. Clitoral vibrators are typically much smaller and are best for people who like direct clitoral stimulation

Dildos are meant to simulate penile penetration. They can be any length or girth – there are ones that are two inches and ones that are monster-sized. People who enjoy the feeling of being penetrated or like the feeling of fullness in their vagina or anus might enjoy dildo play. Be careful when using sex toys. Master your technique of oral first, and then add them in as a side dish. Make sure you don't upset the whole experience by trying to make the sex toy the focus, and make sure she is comfortable with the use of the toy. As with everything, personal hygiene and cleaning of sex toys directly after use is recommended.

Butt plugs stimulate the ring of nerves around the anus. The difference between using butt plug and using a dildo is where a dildo goes in and out, the butt plug just stays in and gives a sustained feeling of fullness. The rabbit toy is a combo of an external vibrator and a G-spot toy. It has an external part that usually looks like rabbit ears that provides vibration to the clitoris, while a second attachment goes inside the vagina for G-spot stimulation so you get double the sensation. Anal beads are another interesting toy.

Unlike butt plugs, which typically go in and stay in, anal beads provide the sensation of the anal sphincter opening and closing. Pulling them out as you orgasm can create a more intense orgasm.

Female Genital Overview

Everything is fair game, so try out all the techniques on all these Key areas.

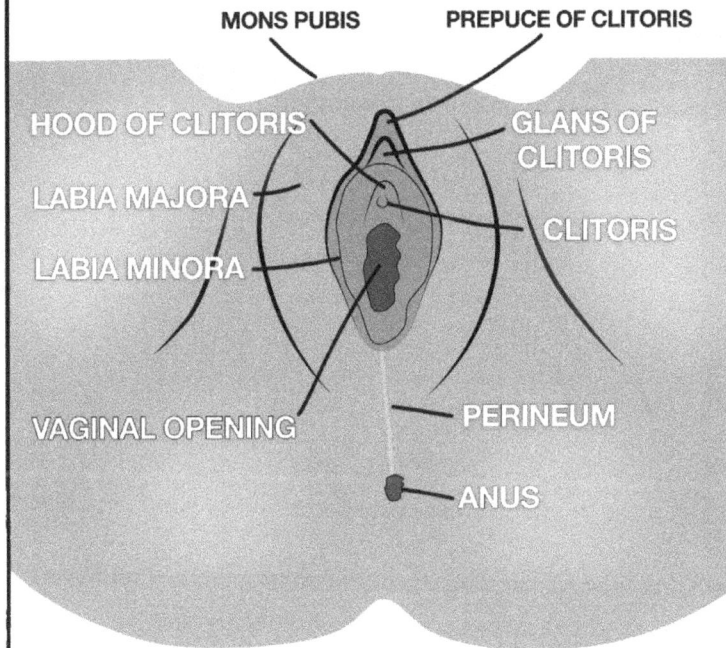

MONS PUBIS   PREPUCE OF CLITORIS

HOOD OF CLITORIS   GLANS OF CLITORIS

LABIA MAJORA

LABIA MINORA   CLITORIS

VAGINAL OPENING   PERINEUM

ANUS

These are the Key External Genital Organs that you should be aware of when performing oral sex.

Marisa Rudder

LYING BACK

POSITION 1

CHAPTER 5

Oral Sex by Numbers | Position #1 – Lying Back

This position is the oral sex equivalent to the missionary position in intercourse. It is the fallback, the go-to basic position, and will always work for both partners. If you are going to be providing oral sex to a woman and this is your first time or early on in the relationship, I suggest starting here. With this traditional cunnilingus positioning, you as the giver will be in between the woman's legs, facing toward her. Your nose will point toward her belly button, This is a good position to get her comfortable and begin your foreplay. I say foreplay, but oral sex is the main event in female-led relationships. So be prepared for that and think about giving, putting her pleasure first. Her pleasure is your pleasure.

OVERVIEW: Take a deep breath, give her a massage, play some cool music, kiss her, rub her legs and booty, gently rub her crotch when she still has her clothes on, kiss her neck, compliment her, trail kisses from her lips to her neck to her breast and all the way until you get downtown. Simply take a few minutes to warm her up. Eventually, you'll know if she wants you to go downtown slower or faster; just do whatever helps her relax and turns her on.

OVERVIEW: It is important to read a woman's different moods, and this is one of the basic steps when performing oral sex. If she isn't in the mood, then don't force it. Be understanding. Remember, her permission and consent are key. Maybe she is feeling uncomfortable or it's her time of menstruation. And believe it or not, not every lady enjoys oral sex, and some women need a bit of coaxing to get started. Eventually, they love it, but sometimes it's tough to get started. So be patient and understanding. Take your time. Unlike men, women are not switches and will require slow foreplay to gradually turn them on until they are super horny. So how do you get her in the mood for pleasure? Begin by kissing her hand, neck, lips moving slowly down to her chest. Rub her breasts, kiss her tummy and her legs and give her body a light overall massage. Tease her a bit, nuzzle your nose outside her panties. Continue kissing and massaging like you are exploring her body. Simply take a few minutes to warm her up. Eventually, you'll know if she wants you to go downtown slower or faster. Just do whatever helps her relax and turns her on. You are going to slowly move to the vagina area and remove her underwear, beginning with light kisses to the outsides of the vagina only. Continue massaging and moving your hands over her legs and tummy.

The following are **"Oral Sex by Numbers."**

These tips correspond to numbers on the Position 1 diagram and will show you how to get it all rolling step-by-step. So you can simply refer to the numbers on the diagram as I explain which part of the pussy we are talking about and what to do when you get there. So let's go!

1) Only use your lips and your tongue to tease the outer mounds – which is the raised area surrounding the lips and vagina first. A common beginner's mistake is to use your fingers and stick them in her vagina right away. This is a big mistake. Forget about your fingers for now and don't do it. Focus on using your lips and your tongue on the outer lips, which medically are known as the "labia majora." These are the bigger outer mounds (raised areas) surrounding the vagina. You should tease them with soft kisses and gentle licks.

2) The only thing your fingers and hands may possibly be doing is gently rubbing her thighs or legs in the beginning.

3) Once you have spent a few minutes warming her up on the outer lips, you can play with the clitoris with your tongue. Be gentle and move slowly. As I mentioned earlier, this is an extremely sensitive area. Now while I tell you to be gentle while you focus on the clitoris, you can still be kissing and licking her clitoris with passion, but that doesn't mean roughly or too fast. Some men love licking pussy so much that they go absolutely crazy – without feeling the vibe, energy, mood. Calm down, cowboy! It's not a race. A woman wants to feel you, and you need to feel your woman. It is best at first to make sure that you explore carefully, gently kissing and softly licking all around the vagina.

4) I would recommend that you move down from the clit to the inner lips, known to doctors as the "labia minora." These thinner inner lips should be kissed and licked as well. While you are doing that move to the vaginal opening and licking up and down like an ice cream cone in this area, gently and slowly is good, so you can sense what she likes. You can always increase

intensity. If you hear her moan or she moves with a writhing pleasure, then you can repeat the motion until she stops. Repetition is a good thing here, especially when you hit on something she likes. Keep doing it because stopping it could stop her progress toward her first orgasm. As she starts nearing orgasm, there's one thing above all else: do not change what you're doing in terms of routine and pacing. Do not let yourself get sped up by her rising intensity. Remain consistent, deliberate, and methodical. Consistency is key for most women, so once you've found something that works, stick to it and do not stray from the path! If you do, you may have a very frustrated woman on your hands. Once she orgasms, let her have a chance to cool down and settle back in before attempting any more action. Tell her how much you enjoy her beautiful body and her beautiful orgasm.

5) Now I also want to advise you not to finger her anus the first time or even the first couple of times you have sex with her. Once you have made love several times, ask her what she thinks about anal sex – orally and otherwise – and take it from her answer about how you should proceed. Trust me, less is more, so follow these wise words in the beginning: No, no, no. Do not touch her anus at all in the early sessions. I'm serious, this is really good advice and not following it could ruin your early oral sex experiences immediately and get you thrown out of her bed.

Oral Sex by Numbers
Lying Back

2. Rub Thighs with Hands

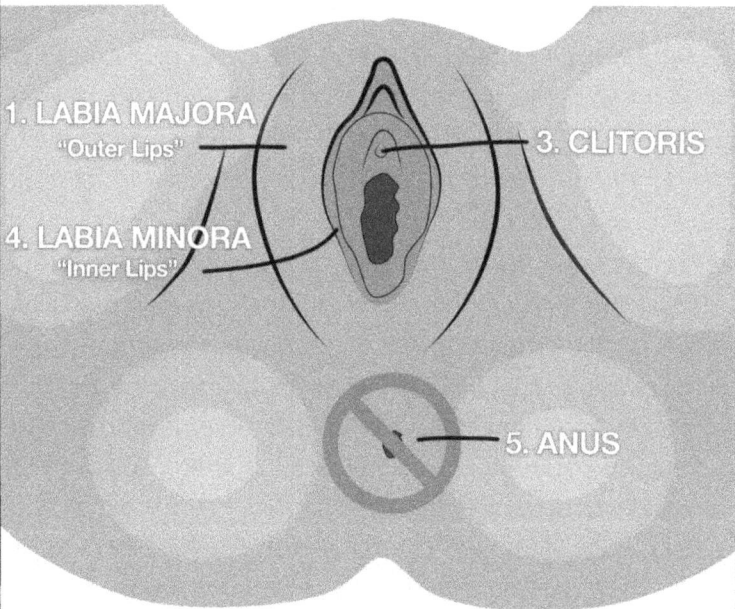

1. LABIA MAJORA
"Outer Lips"

3. CLITORIS

4. LABIA MINORA
"Inner Lips"

5. ANUS

Note: This is the fundamental oral sex position and you will add techniques as you learn.

Position 1

POSITION
2

FORWARD FACESITTING

CHAPTER **6**

Oral Sex by Numbers | Position #2 – Forward Face-Sitting

I f a woman wants to jump right into this position, she wants 100 percent of your focus on her pussy, and she wants her pussy to have its way with your face. Are you ready to have your face fucked, because that's what is about to happen. Since the Love & Obey movement is all about female-led relationships, many women love being on top. Most FLR men love the idea of being able to give a woman pleasure, and this position really emphasizes the whole dom/sub dynamic. When a woman likes face-sitting, you know she wants to ride your face and come. This is a very female dominant position, and she may also be interested in asserting her power and control over you with this position.

Face-sitting is where a woman sits on a man's face. We're talking direct overpowering pussy-to-face contact here. We're talking delightfully smothering intimate oral sex in a very sexy female dominant way. Face-sitting is most commonly used by women who enjoy creating positions of dominance in the sexual power dynamic. This is a parallel dynamic to the woman on top in intercourse. A woman sitting on your face gives her the same control as when she's riding you "cowgirl style." She can control where the pressure goes, she can grind the way she likes, and easily switch between clit, vagina lips, or ass sucking. This is your chance to just sit back and let her take control. You can help by moving the motion with your hands on the thighs.

Oral Sex by Numbers:

1) If she is an aggressive face rider, she will rub her vagina on your face sliding up and down from your chin to your forehead, mainly focusing on your mouth to your nose area. Your job will primarily be to stick your tongue in her vagina and lick around in there as she rides. As you use your tongue in her vagina, your nose – yes your nose – will become a great "penis substitute" for her to rub back and forth against her clit until she orgasms. Maybe that's why women don't mind men with big noses, hmmm. I will warn you that breathing is the trickiest part. You will need to catch your breath every chance you get. There's a reason face-sitting is also known as smothering. It will literally take your breath away. So as she's moving, if she lifts up – even for a moment – grab a breath. This position is a wild ride, to say the least.

2) If she is softer and likes to sit still or gently rock back and forth, you can suck her clit until she loses control and orgasms all over your face. Suck on her clit with your lips and use your tongue inside your lips to gently lick the tip of the clit while your lips are wrapped around it. This is a powerful position for the woman and a submissive position for the man. Your face is being taken and used by a woman's pussy. There will be a real sense of the erotic when you focus on pleasing

her with everything from your mouth to your nose and she explodes on your face in an orgasm.

3) Proceed. This face-sitting position is hands down my favorite, and I like a slow ride so my partner can enjoy all of it. While there are many varied reasons why women enjoy this position, it *is* all about her pleasure and the feeling of complete power. As we have discussed, clitoral stimulation provides the most intense form of pleasure for a woman and the highest probability of orgasm. And this is a position which offers direct stimulation, plus the woman is in control of the motion. Feel free to massage her thighs, butt, breasts, anything to enhance the sensations.

Oral Sex by Numbers
Forward Facesitting

3. Rub Her Legs, Butt and Breasts

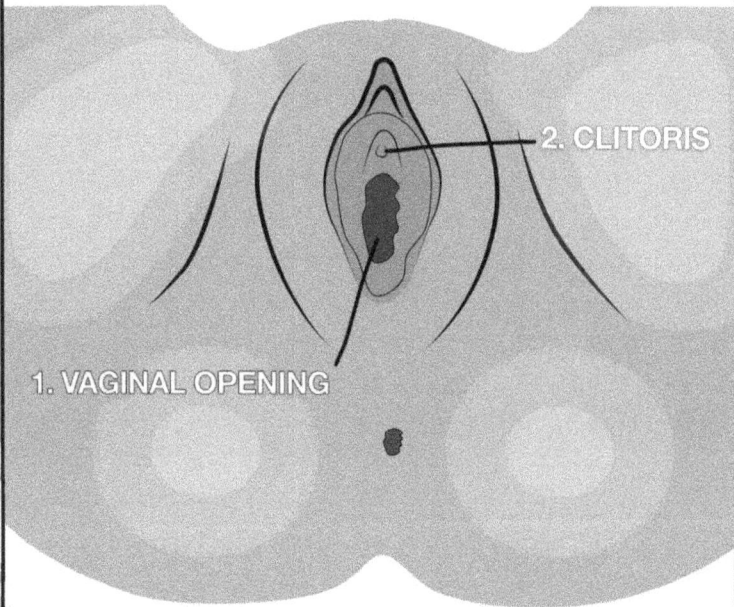

2. CLITORIS

1. VAGINAL OPENING

Note: This is all about letting her use your nose and tongue. Keep on licking.

Position 2

Marisa Rudder

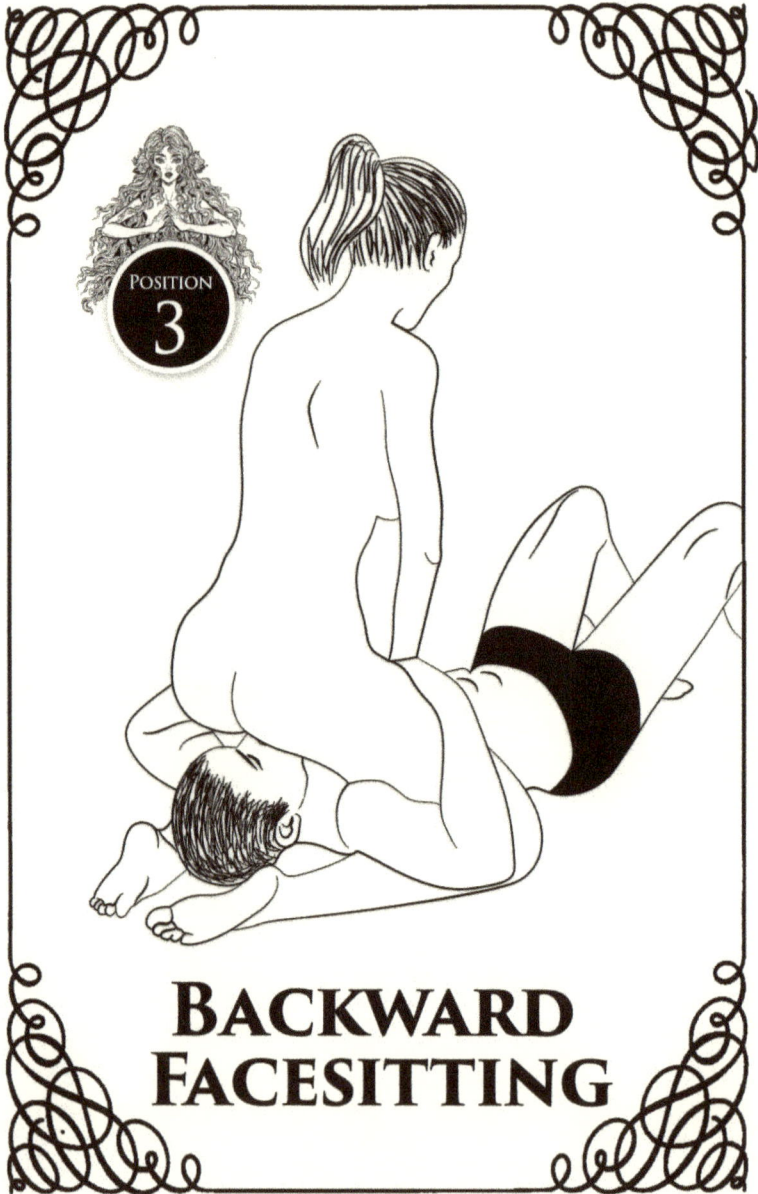

POSITION 3

BACKWARD FACESITTING

48

CHAPTER 7

Oral Sex by Numbers | Position #3
Backward Face-Sitting

If you just thought, this position looks just like the other one, you're correct. Everything that I told you to do in forward face-sitting can also be done in this backward face-sitting, so I'm not going to list all the points again. Face-sitting in either direction is one of the wildest rides in the oral sex amusement park. So think of this a rollercoaster where you sit backward. There are a couple of big differences with the backward face-sitting position. Although the woman is dominant and sitting on your face, sometimes she may also want to suck your dick. As you may have noticed in this face-sitting diagram, the woman faces your dick, and this position is really good, especially if you both want to end up in a 69 position. But again, it may also be that she just likes this direction better and has no interest in 69ing. If she wants it, it's easy for her to bend over a little and get it. Don't push it. You are here to serve her. Her pleasure is your pleasure. Face-sitting also has the nickname "queening" because it is a reminder that she is the queen and your face is her throne. As the man in this position, you will basically lie back and have your face fucked by your woman's pussy. The women is in charge in this type of oral sex, and she runs the show. For most men there is an instant attraction to the power shift and the woman being in control. In terms of either face-sitting direction, women have to be secure and somewhat dominant to choose these positions. As a woman becomes more confident, face-sitting is something she will enjoy doing more often. Some women who are experienced and know what they want love face-sitting. So enjoy bringing her to this way. Now look below because there are a couple of points I want to mention that are specific to this direction. This backward face-sitting is not only about the clit, licking vagina lips, and 69ing. It is a really great position for ass sucking.

Oral Sex by Numbers:

1) One big reason women also like this backward direction is because they really want you to focus on their butt and give them a full lick from vagina to anus. This position is great for ass sucking, and it almost always involves rimming. You will most definitely end up licking all the way from her pussy to her ass as she is moving and riding up and down your face.

2) Obviously, personal hygiene is important when it comes to this position, and washing up before and after is recommended. This is your chance to add a sexy shower as foreplay. If you and your queen are new to this, then experiment with what makes her feel comfortable. This is the added benefit of reading the book together. You can decide what is best for both of you. I'm a big fan of face-sitting men, which is part and parcel of me having a deep love for receiving oral pleasure from a man. If you do it right, your woman will also love face-sitting you. For me, face-sitting is about ensuring maximum pleasure for the goddess while

reinforcing the male's submissive gentlemanly behavior toward me and my dominance over him as his loving female authority.

3) In this position, enjoy the rear view. Massage, caress, and tease as much as you can. Run your hands down her back. Help her to ride you, if she needs it. Ensure your neck is in a comfortable place, and make sure she balances on her knees. I do not recommend being on the feet for this, in case of loss of balance.

Marisa Rudder

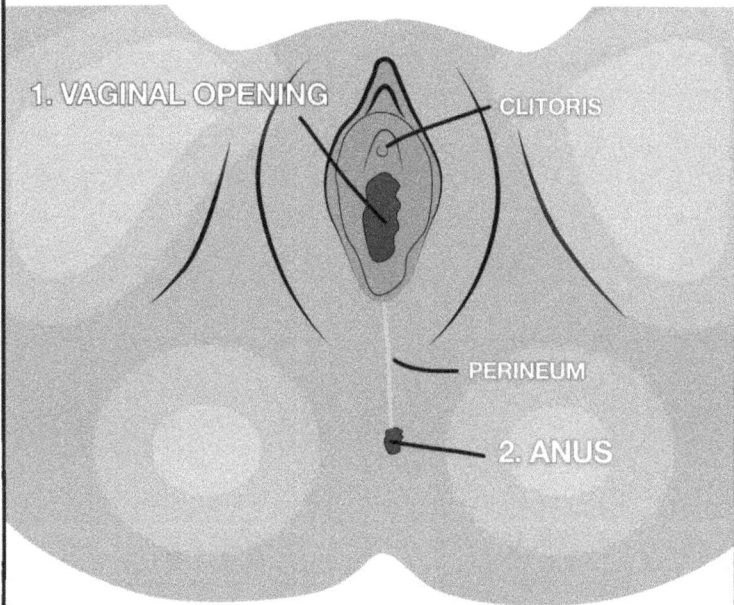

**Oral Sex by Numbers
Backward Facesitting**

3. Rub Her Stomach and Thighs

1. VAGINAL OPENING

CLITORIS

PERINEUM

2. ANUS

**Note: You will be licking the Clitoris
& complete length of Vagina to the
Anus which involves the Perineum.**

Position 3

Marisa Rudder

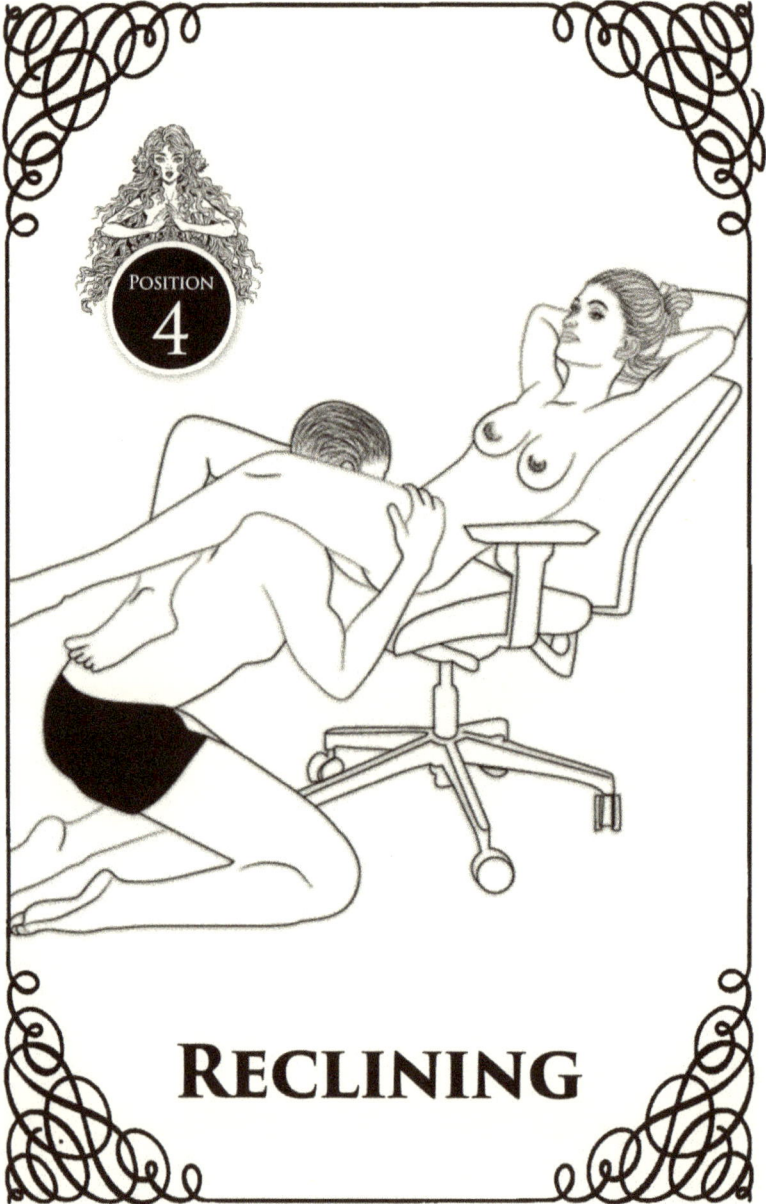

POSITION
4

RECLINING

CHAPTER 8

Oral Sex By Numbers | Position #4 –
R eclining

Reclining is a great way to add to the excitement. Now your goddess can see your every move, and now it's your time to perform and impress. Make sure you both are comfortable. Nothing is worse than kneeling and ending up with a cramp or back pain.

Ensure you begin gently. Because this is sitting up, she may not be in the mood immediately and will need a bit of foreplay. Begin with kissing her feet, moving up her legs. Take your time. Leg massages are so great. Move ever so slowly, making sure you massage her legs all the way up to the vagina. You can even spend some time on the stomach and breasts before moving to the vagina.

Oral Sex by Numbers:

1) Start giving licks and kisses to her vagina, and then move in. The golden rule is never to start with the clitoris. So let's introduce a new technique: Start by

kissing outside the vagina first. Kiss her outer thigh, and work down to the vagina again. Pass the clit and kiss around the vagina. Kiss the outer lips (labia majora) and try little gentle love nibbles here and there – some women don't love it, and please DON'T BITE; this area is very sensitive. Lick up from the bottom of the vagina opening to the bottom of her clit and flick your tongue over her clitoris. You can identify the clitoris in this illustration. At this point she should be ready for some attention on her clit.

2) Once you have arrived at the goddess's pleasure palace, try the circular technique. Slowly begin tracing circles around her clitoris with your tongue. Make sure your movements are slow, steady, and rhythmic. You must use very light, slow circles. Pretend your tongue is as light as a feather when you first begin. As her pleasure increases, begin to use more tongue weight and flick the hood of her clitoris up and down like you are teasing it. Remember, the clitoris has approximately eight thousand sensory nerve endings, so always be gentle. Then go back to tracing circles. Every so often flick your tongue up and down again like you're licking an ice cream cone on the clit and see how she responds. If she likes it, then begin doing it a little more often. If she doesn't, then immediately stop and continue tracing circles. Allow her to move freely, but try to keep the same pace and rhythm. Keep the pace steady. If she wants more pressure, she will likely gyrate her pussy to get more. She may even grab your head at this point to keep it where she wants it. Remember, once she is gyrating or holding you to a position, never remove your mouth from the clit. I repeat, don't stop till she orgasms or asks you to do something else.

3) At this point, you are probably nearing her orgasm, and all the focus is on the clitoris. The size of her clitoris varies just like the size of the penis. If she has a larger clitoris, she may want more pressure and possibly want your tongue exploring all around the edges of her clit. If it is smaller, she may want much softer strokes. There are basically three things you do to the clitoris. Kiss it, lick it, and suck it. Some women love having the clitoris sucked, especially if it's a good-sized clit. Others, typically those with smaller clits, just love you licking, and they may want nothing more than the tip of your tongue on the clit if they are super sensitive. As she approaches orgasm, consistency matters. Keep the same rhythm and speed that is exciting her. Be aware of her as she squirms, bites her lip, moans or groans, grabs your head or moves her hips, grabs the bed sheets, or starts verbalizing, "Fuck yes, right there!" Any of the above-mentioned are signs that you are doing it right. So keep doing it the same, the same pace and rhythm. Don't be tempted to go faster because she is getting more excited. Women love to focus on where the pleasure is coming from, so change can set you back to zero and ruin her orgasm. So when the captain of a ship is on the right course, he says, "Steady as she goes!" Now as her sex captain, you can say, "STEADY AS SHE BLOWS!" This is the simplest rule to follow to bring her to orgasm right. Trust me, she will orgasm so intensely she won't able to walk for the next twenty minutes!

Oral Sex by Numbers
Reclining

**1. Start by Kissing the Thighs
and the Outer Areas of the Vagina.**

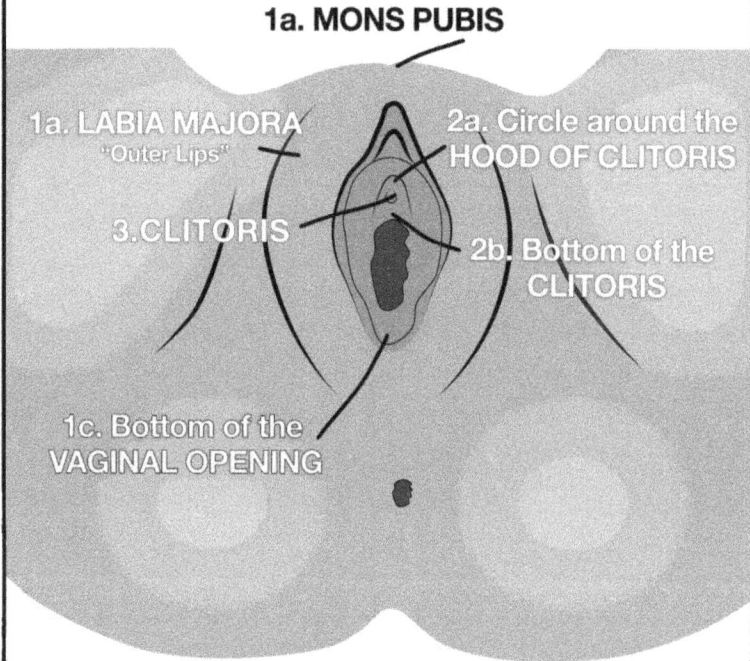

1a. MONS PUBIS

1a. LABIA MAJORA
"Outer Lips"

2a. Circle around the
HOOD OF CLITORIS

3. CLITORIS

2b. Bottom of the
CLITORIS

1c. Bottom of the
VAGINAL OPENING

**Note: Let her sit back, relax
and enjoy the flight.**

Position 4

Marisa Rudder

LYING SIDEWAYS

POSITION 5

60

CHAPTER 9

Oral Sex by Numbers | Position #5 – Lying Sideways

T he sideways position is different than anything we have discussed before because the male giver actually lies perpendicular to the female. The couple is at a ninety-degree angle, making somewhat of a capital *L* shape with their bodies, as you can see in the illustration. So instead of looking up at the clit as you have been in the other positions, you're looking at it sideways. You can experiment with coming in from either the left or right side of your woman. Why? Some women will tell you that one side of their clit is more sensitive than the other, so it's a good idea to try both sides and ask them which side delivers more magic. Begin with massaging the legs, the pubic area, and the butt to get her comfortable and warmed up.

Oral Sex by Numbers:

1) Now that you're in position, do some licking warm-ups on that beautiful vagina. The fun part of this position is that you're licking horizontally (instead of the usual vertical direction) across the hood of the clit in a gentle up and down motion, much like you'd eat an ice cream cone. A delicious and snazzy movement. For some reason in this sideways position, some men say that when the clitoris gets aroused, they can feel a small bump on either side of the clitoral hood, something like a grain of rice. If you are able to feel it, try sweeping your tongue over the clitoral hood and in between these two points. Remember that the clitoral tissue swells, just like a penis. So keep your eye and tongue alert, and you might notice these tiny bumps during the experience. Of course, everyone's genitals are unique, and some women may not have them. Don't worry if you can't find them. She will be able to orgasm with or without them.

2) Now for the first time we are going to introduce the fingers. By the way, I will mention that fingers can be used, but this is something to test with each woman and see if she is a fan or not. Anyway, let's try a new technique to master with your hands for this position. With your left hand, place your index finger and thumb on either side of the clitoris to raise it and help keep it exposed to your tongue while you lick. As you are adjusting and setting your finger position, you can ask your woman exactly what finger positioning feels best for her, and adjust accordingly. With your right hand, place gentle pressure on the perineum (see the illustration for the exact position). The perineum is a pleasure gauge, and you will feel involuntary muscle contractions and spasms indicating her pussy likes

what you're doing. This will help you focus in on what feels best for her. No words necessary.

3) Some people find pressure on their perineum uncomfortable. This can easily be solved by inserting a finger into the vaginal canal. Either of these should give you similar feedback, so explore what works best for her. This is mainly just a trick for getting physical feedback. So if she doesn't like either one. You can also get good feedback from observing her gyrations, moans, involuntary muscle movements in her stomach muscles, and breathing patterns. Of course, beyond the physical feedback cues you can simply ask her for and listen to verbal directions and her feedback.

4) Once you are in position and working it, it is crucial for you try a few different variants with your tongue and find out exactly what your partner likes before you get into your "steady-as-she-blows" rhythm. The key in any position is to figure out the different nuances that feel best to your goddess and then "steady as she blows!" So, men, listen up, this is usually pretty important to most women receiving any type of oral sex: once you hit the sweet spot, stay with it. To figure out what works best, check out our clit touch styles.

Oral Sex by Numbers
Lying Sideways

You are licking horizontally in the position.

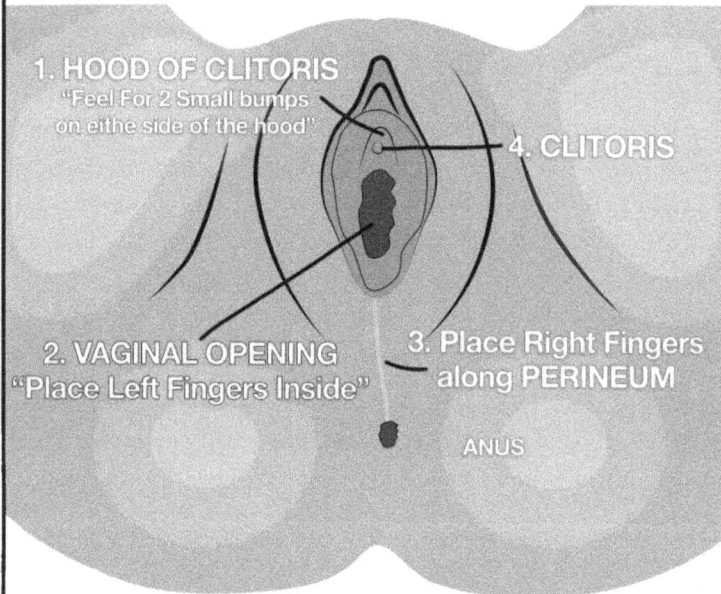

1. HOOD OF CLITORIS
"Feel For 2 Small bumps on eithe side of the hood"

4. CLITORIS

2. VAGINAL OPENING
"Place Left Fingers Inside"

3. Place Right Fingers along PERINEUM

ANUS

Note: This is all about enjoying the new horizontal angle sensations.

Position 5

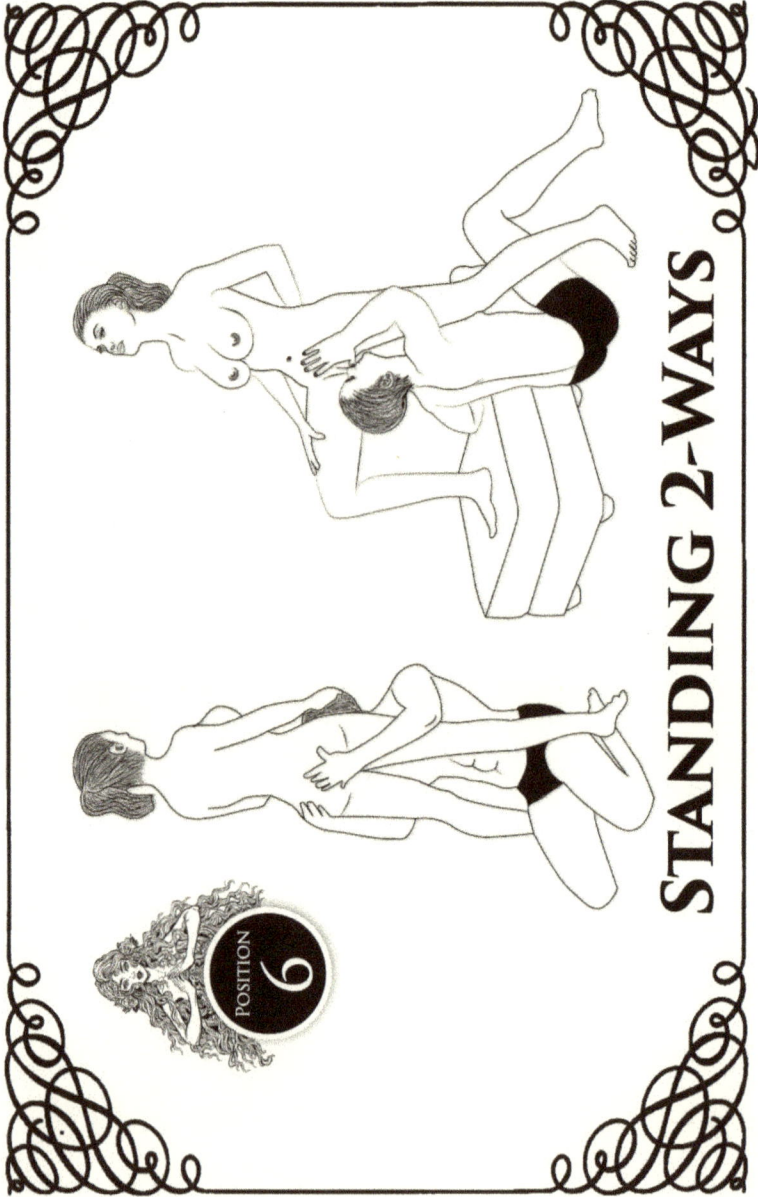

Marisa Rudder

STANDING 2-WAYS

POSITION 6

66

CHAPTER 10

Oral Sex by Numbers | Position #6 – Standing 2-Ways

As the illustration suggests, you can do the standing position flat on the floor or with one foot elevated on a piece of furniture. The standing position can be nice because the man is kneeling before his woman like she is a goddess. It's very ceremonial and allows the woman to assert her dominance and really be in control. Let her know that you love her vagina and that you are dying to give it pleasure. This is also a good position to use your fingers in new ways, so use them, but please don't be all thumbs. In fact, don't use any thumbs. Begin by massing the feet and the ankles, moving up and down the legs, even the butt. Lick the insides of her thighs.

Oral Sex by Numbers:

1) Your woman has probably found proper pleasure from the previous techniques that I have shared with you, like the circular tongue motions. Now let me tell you about another direct type of tongue stimulation of her clitoris. Remember, all women differ in their sensitivity. Your woman probably enjoyed the circular motions I shared with you earlier, but here's another movement you may find is perfect for helping her achieve an orgasm. Instead of using circles around her clitoral shaft, you will now try to lick her clitoris sideways with light strokes of your tongue.

2) Now how about those fingers? First and foremost, don't use your fingers right away, because the famous G-spot is easiest to locate when a woman is aroused. Perform at least five full minutes of using the circular, sideways, or up and down like you're licking a lollipop, or try all of the above techniques first. Once she is getting a bit wiggly, moaning, and breathing heavier, you can now place one or two fingers in her vagina and begin stimulating her G-spot. As I have explained, medical researchers now consider the G-spot to be part of what's known as the clitourethrovaginal (CUV) complex – the interior portion of the clitoris and part of the vaginal wall. It is an area which, stimulated properly, can induce intense orgasms. When the G-spot is aroused, it will feel bumpy, like a small rough patch on her smooth inner vagina wall. This is because the G-spot is composed of erectile tissue, which means it swells up when blood rushes to it. That's why you don't want to rush to find it. Give her at least five minutes of tongue pleasure so the interior clitoral tissue will get aroused and swollen. This sexual arousal will make the area firmer and rougher feeling than the

rest of the smooth surrounding vaginal wall. Once she is aroused, you will generally find the G-spot about two to three inches inside the upper vaginal wall; think of the location being on the backside of the clitoris. However, the location will vary slightly in each woman. So now that you know how to search for the G-spot, let your "Indiana Jones" fingers go exploring and see what kind of "treasure of pleasure" you can discover in that magical vaginal cave you're exploring. When a man successfully finds it and massages it with his finger, it can be one of the most intense types of orgasms a woman can experience, especially if you are gently sucking and licking her clitoris at the same time!

3) As always, you will want to use a steady rhythm. This allows her to mentally focus on the pleasure you are giving her and stay in tempo with you and what you're doing. If you head down there and use your tongue like you're wildly shooting in every direction, she won't become accustomed to her pleasure rhythm, and her pleasure will decrease. Remember, always keep repeating this in your mind, "Steady as she goes." You're the Captain of this pleasure cruise, and if you stay on course, she will orgasm. So give your crew – the lips, tongue, and mouth – your command: "Steady as she blows, mates." That's it, "Steady as she blows!"

4) Now I want to share with you another tip to make cunnilingus easier for you to perform correctly. It's perfectly designed to hit those eight thousand clit nerve endings she has down there. Use this technique as she nears orgasm, and most of the time it'll push her right over the ecstasy cliff. Start at the top of her clitoris and lick her downward until you reach the bottom of her labia, then move straight back up the line you initially came down on. As I mentioned, use this method when

she is already highly aroused and ready to hit her climax. You still want to use "steady as she blows," but this time, increase the pressure you're using. Once again, the amount of pressure you use is always dependent on her sensitivity. Continue moving your tongue up and down like you're licking a lollipop on this line until she orgasms. When her legs begin quivering, her breathing is heavy and you hear her moaning or verbalizing, "Oh yes, oh, oh, oh," you will know she's receiving maximum pleasure and climaxing.

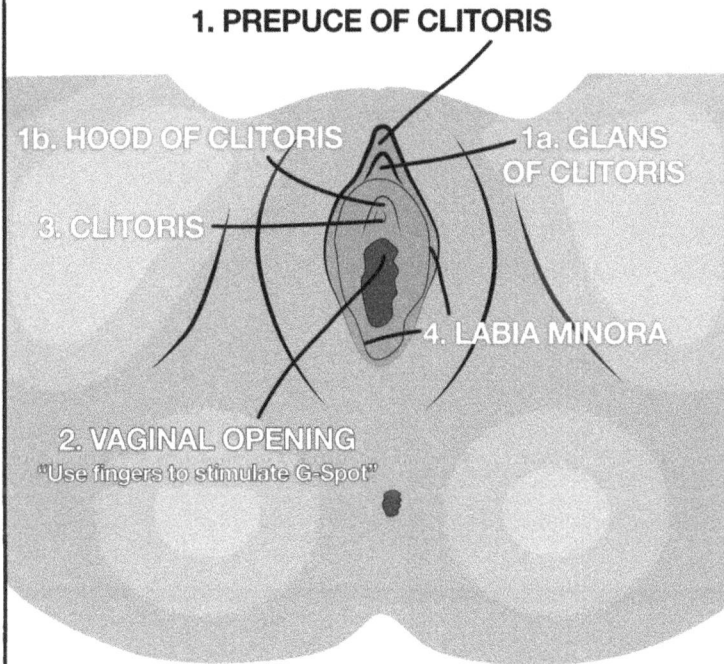

**Oral Sex by Numbers
Standing 2-Ways**

1. PREPUCE OF CLITORIS

1b. HOOD OF CLITORIS

1a. GLANS OF CLITORIS

3. CLITORIS

4. LABIA MINORA

2. VAGINAL OPENING
"Use fingers to stimulate G-Spot"

Note: The "G-Spot" is located inside the
Vagina. It is the interior portion of the Clitoris.

Position 6

Marisa Rudder

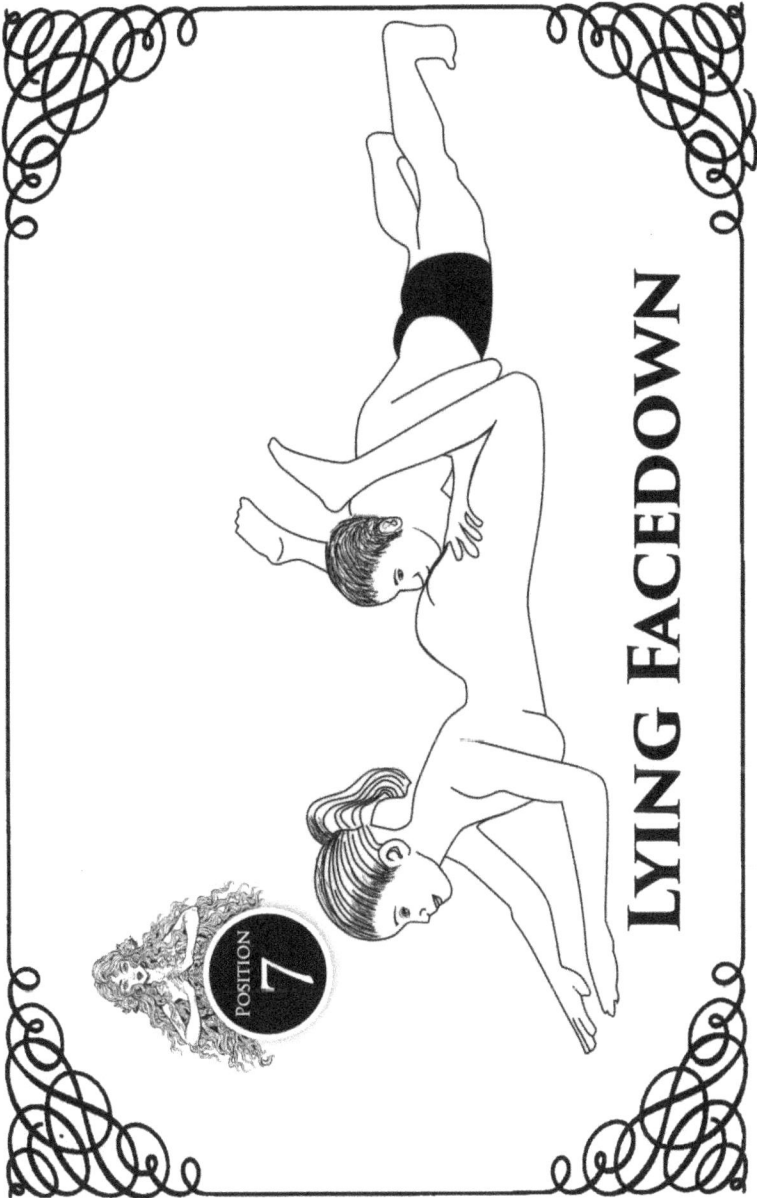

LYING FACEDOWN

POSITION 7

CHAPTER 11

Oral Sex by Numbers | Position #7 –
Lying Facedown

Now we are going to turn off the cunnilingus highway and take the scenic route for a while. Pull over and exit onto the *anilingus* highway. Now be ready for another oral sex adventure. Anilingus, which is also known as *rimming*, is the act of orally pleasuring the anus. This lying-on-the-floor position is perfect for giving your partner a great rim job and can involve licking, sucking, kissing, and any other pleasurable act that involves oral-to-anal contact. Naturally, you can definitely experiment to find other positions that work for you. A modified version of lying on the floor is another very obvious choice, as well as "four on the floor" or doggie style.

No matter how you decide to do it, this can be very exciting, but again, it has to be done with her comfort in mind. She should be lying on her stomach. You can begin getting her in the mood with massage and kisses. This may even be a good opportunity to give her a great massage. She may have to raise her hips up slightly so you can get to the vagina.

IMPORTANT SAFETY MESSAGE: We do need to take a moment to talk about safety and hygiene because like any other sex act, there is some risk involved in any kind of anal touching. Cleanliness is an important part of rimming to prevent the spread of bacteria. Taking a good shower and paying particular attention to your anus before you begin is a good idea. Like all other anal play, you must always think safety. Cleaning and cleanliness is very important. A personal tip for the ladies (guys can suggest and even treat your lady): think about getting a full Brazilian wax and being totally hairless down there. Why worry about how your vagina or anus looks with hair? A bush and hairy anus will most probably be a real turnoff for your partner and can ruin your enjoyment. Maybe this is just one of my personal hang-ups, but I think getting rid of all the hair can help you relax and enjoy the oral sex experience so much more.

Oral Sex by Numbers:

1) To do this, have your goddess get down on her stomach on the bed, either flat or on all fours. You should lie down or kneel behind her. Use your hands to guide her butt up or down to the height that provides you with the best angle for servicing. Use your hands to spread your partner's cheeks. Lying flat and kneeling on all fours are not the only positions for oral/anal sex. The last position we will discuss will actually have the woman stand and bend over while you kneel behind her. She will stand and bend at the waist, and she can hold her ankles if she is limber and in good shape, while you kneel or crouch behind her and provide your services. While lying flat on the floor or bed, a woman can put a pillow under her head for comfort and even one under her pelvic/hip region to raise it up while you kneel behind and between her thighs.

2) The advice that I have given you for good oral sex in all the other positions will also apply in large part to performing good oral/anal sex. Start off slow and work your way to the pleasure spot instead of going in for the kill straight off. Once again, soft, light licks and kisses of the inner thighs and perineum are a great way to start and are sure to get her warmed up for anal action.

3) When you're ready to move to the vagina. You can't go wrong by using your tongue, and I suggest that you lick up and down along the line of her butt crack, just like licking a lollipop or ice cream cone. Remember my basic oral sex techniques and tips, and this time use long, slow licks with your tongue flat against your partner's anus. Experiment with your tongue, alternating between stiffening and relaxing it. Try different directions, such as up and down, and lick it like an ice cream cone but also try some circular and side-to-side motions. After a bit of licking, tighten up your tongue and point it while pushing it against her anus, using enough pressure to gently penetrate the hole. You can also gently rub her clitoris. Penetrate her vagina with your fingers (if you are keeping them out of her ass). You should also caress her neck, back, lower back, and inner thighs. And let's not forget a squeeze or little spanking of her cheeks can add to the fun.

Oral Sex by Numbers
Lying Facedown

Focus is on her Anus

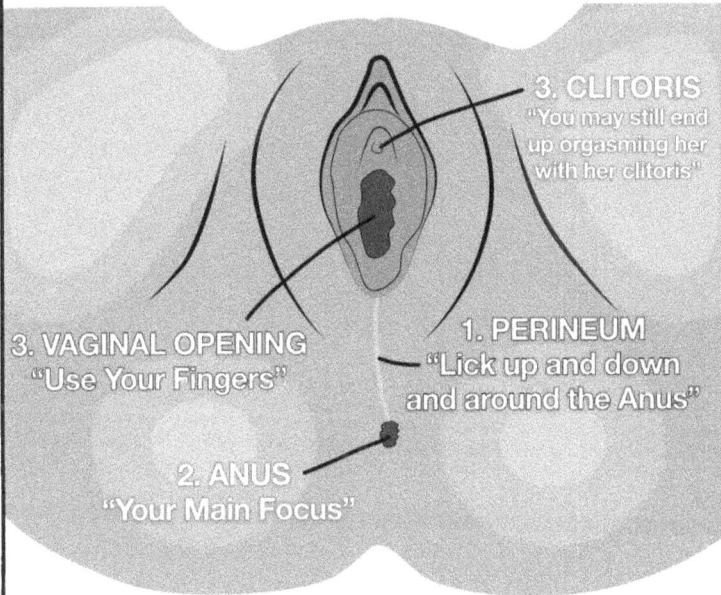

3. CLITORIS
"You may still end up orgasming her with her clitoris"

3. VAGINAL OPENING
"Use Your Fingers"

1. PERINEUM
"Lick up and down and around the Anus"

2. ANUS
"Your Main Focus"

Note: You can rub her back, lower back and inner thighs.

Position 7

Marisa Rudder

SEATED REVERSE

POSITION 8

CHAPTER 12

Oral Sex by Numbers | Position #8 – Seated Reverse

This position may work better for women and men in good shape physically who are not in danger of any head or brain conditions. Please ensure you have a clean bill of health and you have been in this position before, like during Yoga or other exercise. Make sure your neck placement is comfortable. If you feel any pain or discomfort, stop immediately. But if you can do it, it's great because it allows you great visual access to the beauty of that spectacular pussy. Using a pillow, yoga mat, or carpeted floor and getting comfortable is important for your woman so she can feel good and relax. You will be comfortable because you get to sit down and perform this oral sex position. Once you find a good place to do this, you can enjoy the view and get started.

Oral Sex by Numbers:

1) Once you are in the position, again, making her feel comfortable is very important. Ensure you are in a comfortable position and you have the flexibility in your back.

2) Begin again with massages and kisses to the outside of the vagina, and then move in as described previously. Now you can really massage her stomach and even her breasts if you can reach. What's exciting about this is the feeling of doing an acrobatic move like you're in Cirque du Soleil. It's also a great switch-up.

3) Get the fingers and hands involved. They should be part of the fun. While your mouth is on her clit, trace your index finger to her vagina (see why I told you to cut those nails), insert it in slowly (about two inches), and gently pull the vagina down. This makes the vagina feels like there is a penis in it, and the brain sends more blood to the walls to heighten sensitivity. The G-spot should be swelling by now.

4) Turn your index finger up and make what I call the "cum sign." It is like the gesture you would make with your finger if you were signaling someone to come over to you. Continue making the "cum sign" and licking the clitoris simultaneously. You are going to blow her mind; feel it as her reaction increases. You can also use two fingers if she likes that better. When you are going to use two fingers to stimulate her, do not turn the fingers while they are still inside her vagina. You are trying to give her pleasure. Turning your fingers inside her vagina can hurt and even tear her vaginal walls. Remember, this is a very sensitive area. Simply pull your fingers out a little and turn them before you insert them again. Remember, the G-spot is about two inches

up the wall. Now start making the "cum sign." If she isn't into it, she will probably push your hand away or say no fingers. If that's the case, let your tongue take over. Your other hand should be exploring her body: massage her breasts, squeeze them gently, rub the nipple, use your hands all over her body. Great tongue, great fingering, and great massaging hands equal a great orgasm!

Oral Sex by Numbers
Seated Reverse

1. Get Comfortable with Her Kissing her Stomach, Lower Abdomen and MONS PUBIS.

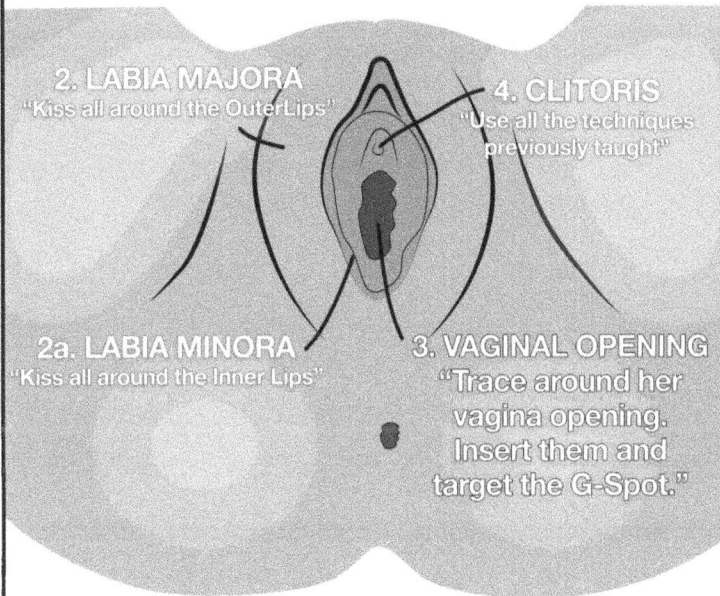

2. LABIA MAJORA
"Kiss all around the OuterLips"

4. CLITORIS
"Use all the techniques previously taught"

2a. LABIA MINORA
"Kiss all around the Inner Lips"

3. VAGINAL OPENING
"Trace around her vagina opening. Insert them and target the G-Spot."

Note: This is a great position for rubbing the G-SPOT while kissing, licking or sucking the Clitoris.

Position 8

Marisa Rudder

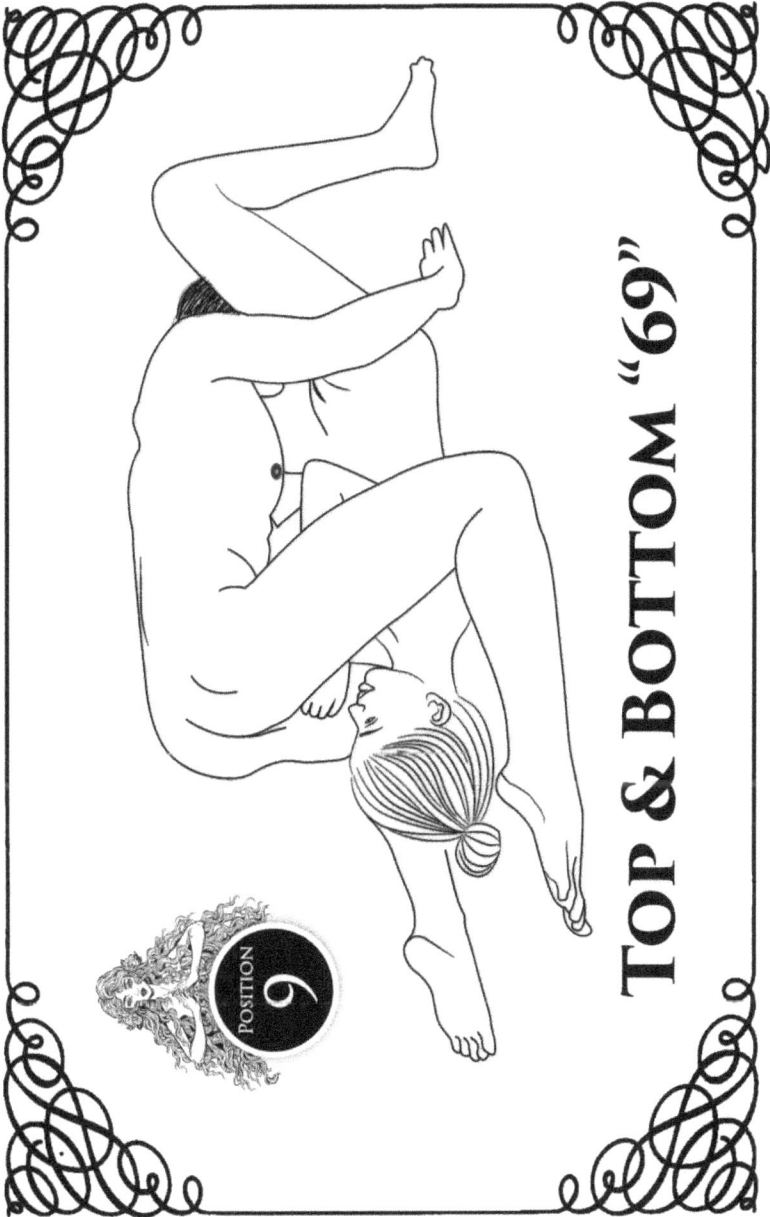

TOP & BOTTOM "69"

POSITION 9

CHAPTER **13**

Oral Sex by Numbers | Position #9 –
Top and Bottom

The secret to 69ing like a champion is to have fun with it. This is a great relaxing opportunity to get to know each other's bodies better and which sensations work and don't work for you both. So before, during, and after going down on each other, keep it relaxed, communicate, and keep it fun and sexy. I like the top and bottom 69 position because the woman is comfortable and relaxed, and the man is in a great position to service her whole body. You can both easily communicate with each other, and you can both learn in a fun way. For example, have your woman lie on a rug or bed. Kneel on the down her body until you're both in the 69 position. At any point along the way, she can tell you or you can ask what she likes and what feels good to her and vice-versa. One of the great things about the 69 is that there's plenty of body to explore and you can take your time to get to know each other. Massaging and talking with her can also be put to good use when your mouth needs a break.

1) In the 69 position, your hands can deliver a great deal of pleasure to all her pubic area hot spots, such as her mons pubis and her perineum. I just mentioned the mons pubis. Do you know the mons pubis? Let me introduce you. It may sound weird, but gently tugging on her mons pubis with your hands can feel amazing. Why, because it's connected to the hood of the clitoris and her lips, labia majora and minora. Simply pulling on it in an up-and-down motion can stroke the internal shaft of her clitoris. Once aroused, your woman may find that stroking the clitoris indirectly by pulling on the mons pubis feels super hot, maybe even as hot as direct stimulation of her clitoris. Simple strokes of the mons pubis can stimulate her pubic area in a crazy-sexy-hot way. Try varying the intensity and length of your massaging or kneading movement or ask your woman what feels good to her. Let her help you focus on the sensations of being touched that work best for her. When you are both focusing on how it feels to be touched in a certain way, you will both have a better understanding of what turns her on, ultimately leading to better sex and stronger orgasms.

2) It's great to put this concept to use during 69ing because it is interactive two-party oral sex. You can both focus and comment on what it feels like to touch, kiss, lick, and be touched, licked, and kissed in certain places. This will allow you both to get to know each other better. Take a moment to trace your woman's body parts with your fingers, like the curve of her breasts or pubic area, instead of just going after them immediately with your mouth. If you're planning to make the 69 position your main event, another great way to do it is for both of you to lie on your side. You can also switch it up so you won't have to worry about

muscle fatigue and can keep any neck or body pain to a minimum.

3) Remember, have fun and communicate. Ask her if she likes it when you go slow, go fast, go in circles, go in long strokes, change up the pressure and suction. Make it fun and create a unique experience every time. Remember, one of the most important and fundamental psychological issues of oral sex: the hottest oral sex is when your woman feels like you're really enjoying going down on her, just like it turns you on when you feel like your woman is really enjoying the sensation of giving you a blow job. Nobody can fully enjoy oral sex unless they know their partner is enjoying it as well.

Oral Sex by Numbers
Top and Bottom "69"

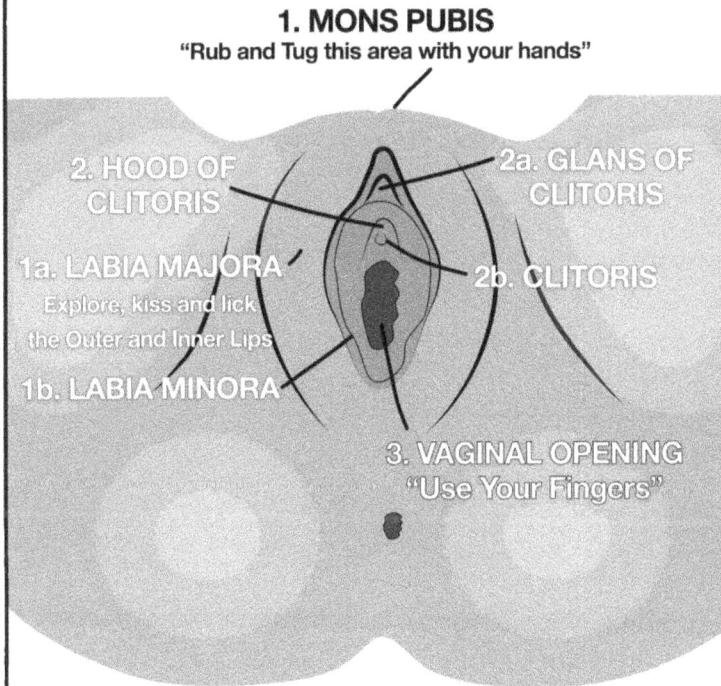

1. MONS PUBIS
"Rub and Tug this area with your hands"

2. HOOD OF CLITORIS

2a. GLANS OF CLITORIS

1a. LABIA MAJORA
Explore, kiss and lick the Outer and Inner Lips

2b. CLITORIS

1b. LABIA MINORA

3. VAGINAL OPENING
"Use Your Fingers"

Note: This is an excellent position for mutual genital area exploration.

Position 9

Marisa Rudder

POSITION
10

BENT &
BEHIND

CHAPTER 14

Oral Sex by Numbers | Position #10 – Bent and Behind

This position is very exciting. Full and complete exposure of her vagina and butt make it easy access. The negative is that she has to stand on her feet and be bent over in what can become a tiring or uncomfortable position in the long run.

However, it can be extremely visually exciting and stimulating for shorter periods of time. For this reason, you can use just about any and all of the tips and techniques I have shared with you in the previous nine positions. You can tantalize her vagina, you can tease her butt, you can finger and kiss and suck at will. You can do it all enjoying a great view of your beautiful goddess's most divine erogenous zone. So instead of offering specifics, I am going to use this position to recap the highlights of what we have learned so far and offer some common-sense advice to make your oral sex experiences pleasurable for your woman.

1) Keep her knees bent so she doesn't lose her balance.

2) Give her compliments. "I love your pussy." "I think it's beautiful." "It smells so sexy." "I love the taste." "I've been dreaming about this moment." "I can't wait to taste you." "I want to keep licking you and my fingers because you taste incredible." Many women feel insecure about the beauty, smell, and taste of their pussies. Complimenting her pussy and telling her in your own sincere words that you think her pussy looks beautiful, smells great, and tastes delicious is a sure-fire way to get her relaxed and make the experience more pleasurable for you both.

3) Massage and kiss the whole body. It really enhances the mood.

4) Don't be afraid to ask her to guide you, tell you what turns her on and turns her off. Continue as long as she is comfortable, but if she is tired or in pain, it's time to switch it up.

5) Do not skip foreplay. Warm her up with kisses and caresses all over her body. Be patient; eventually, you will get to go down there. Spend some quality time getting her warmed up, and you can have a much better experience when you get to the pleasure palace. Tease her as much as you can.

6) Remember, once you're on the right course, be like a ship's captain and command your tongue and the rest of your crew, "Steady as she blows." Don't try to rush the whole orgasm thing, or you will ruin everything. You are not trying to win a race or reach a goal as fast as possible. You are not trying to prove a point. Just relax so she will relax and enjoy the journey. If she is

having a harder time getting over the edge and climaxing, you may try increasing or decreasing the speed and pressure a little. But once you feel any wriggling, hear any moaning, or have her grab your head, always remember one thing: "Steady as she blows." Don't stop until she is finished or she flat out tells you she is fully satisfied and wants a good fuck!

7) Remember, hands and fingers are involved unless she doesn't like it. Get a manicure and keep those nails well-groomed and clean. The lips, mouth, and tongue are your main tools of choice in getting the job done, but your fingers can and do play a role. Introduce them slowly and see how she responds. Some women love it, and some women don't. Always read her reactions.

8) If she isn't communicating, you should simply ask her. Tell her you want to learn about her desires and preferences. Ask her to help you out and give you direction. Understand that women don't like just to tell you what they want; they do enjoy giving you clues. They like to see if you are intelligent, perceptive; and interested enough to pay attention. So pay attention to verbal and non-verbal messaging. Is she wiggling around, is she breathing heavy, is she moaning? If she doesn't give any directions or you don't get any physical clues, maybe her message is simply she is not in the mood.

9) The bedroom or sitting room is a place for adventure, and you should be like Indiana Jones, a great explorer. Search her body and your bag of tricks to see what gets you to the treasure in her pleasure cave and what gets you lost. Have fun, and be sensitive to her body messaging. Play with all of her other senses: sight, smell, hearing, taste, and touch. Also, I just gave you

ten oral sex positions: try them all out and see what she likes. You can even use props, handcuffs, whips, and sex toys if you have them to spice it up.

10) Finally, the clitoris is your mission, your target; your focus is ultimately always the clit. While it is good to focus on other parts till you get there, once you get to the clit, this becomes the goal of your mission – lock onto it with your lips, tongue, and mouth, and don't move anywhere else. Show her you love it and be passionate about the way you kiss, lick, and suck it. Eight thousand nerves guaranteed to drive her wild!

Marisa Rudder

Oral Sex by Numbers
Bent and from Behind

Everything is fair game, so try out all the techniques on all the key areas.

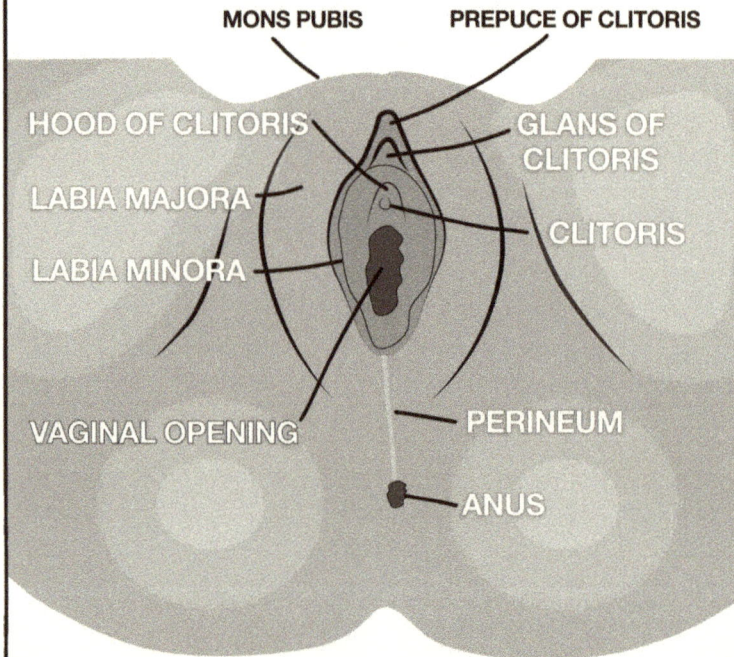

MONS PUBIS   PREPUCE OF CLITORIS

HOOD OF CLITORIS   GLANS OF CLITORIS

LABIA MAJORA   CLITORIS

LABIA MINORA

VAGINAL OPENING   PERINEUM

ANUS

Note: This position is very revealing so start off with compliments to relax her. good advice for every position.

Position 10

96

CHAPTER 15

Now that you have all the specifics about how to perform oral sex on your goddess, it is time to consider how you will add it into the relationship. Women in female-led relationships are powerful and defiant; they have rejected the ideas of the patriarchal system. These modern, liberated women are designing the type of female-led life that they want to live. I call these women the Love & Obey women. Their social status has nothing to do with money. The Love & Obey woman knows what she wants, and most, if not all, of the time, she gets it. Boredom, burnout, depression, and even chronic frustration are not conditions she is willing to put up with in her life. I am this type of woman, and I have known many women like this for more than a decade now. I wrote my first book, *Love & Obey*, about how to create the perfect female-led relationship. If you are with a woman who enjoys oral sex but you want her to be more take charge to create the ultimate female-led relationship, this is how you do it. Improving the sex life is one of the most important steps in improving relationships because it is the first to go downhill. Studies show that more than 50 percent of couples in a relationship longer than six months, according to Zavamed, experienced a decline in frequency of sex, but 59 percent of women said they wanted more sex. The most cited reasons for less sex were being too busy, being stressed, lack of time, lack of intimacy, lack of communication about sex and children.

So one of the biggest changes you will need to make in a female-led relationship is to attempt to deal with these issues with open communication with your queen and by supporting her in general daily duties, so that you both have the time and energy for sex. Sex has to be placed in your routine, similar to date night and weekends away. This is very important to the success of the relationship, but it gives you an opportunity to take over the planning of these exciting times to surprise your queen and make sure they happen. Leaders cannot function without support staff. Your queen cannot function without your support. You will need to set aside time for communication and for quality time away from stressors. I often suggest to couples that the man get involved in the planning of these events as women often are handling so much at work and a home, they simply do not have the time nor the energy to do it. In addition, I have heard numerous complaints from women about men never planning weekend getaways or surprises for them. Men, your women notice these things, so get on it. Men need to show involvement in showing their eagerness to keep the excitement alive; then your queen will respond by being a willing participant. If you are trying to create a perfect female-led relationship and empower your queen, you need to begin by constantly asking her what she wants to do. I had the delightful experience of my partner asking me if he could have a drink at dinner. Just that simple request made me know that he held me as his goddess supreme. It's is a small thing but a simple thing – when you empower your queen in simple things, she becomes empowered for even bigger things. I was very impressed when a couple I knew who was on the brink of divorce turned everything around by creating a female-led relationship. She began to take charge more than she had in a decade – making her husband do all the things she knew she had no time for, and he stepped up and became her support system. She insisted that they take up fitness together, boating, and attending networking events, and through all of this, they not only became fitter and more successful at meeting people, but the relationship changed dramatically. He saw her as sexy again and was turned on with her take-charge attitude, and she was happier making more money, being fitter, and feeling more supported and relaxed. This is the power of a female-led relationship.

I discovered the common traits of many females who take charge – the Love & Obey women. It turns out these women follow a set of strategies and principles. If you are with this type of woman, you will be performing a great deal of oral sex because you must show your service and devotion in all things, in and outside the bedroom. The sex is the center. Both of you recharge with the release of sexual pleasure: you both deepen your intimate connection, and you prevent the decline of the relationship. In addition, for those couples who fear infidelity, if you are satisfying your goddess with her as the focus, she's not going outside for more, and neither are you. Cheating can be disastrous for a relationship. The lying, the hiding, the introduction of outside people and factors into what is supposed to be a committed union can lead to destruction. It is important that couples work on strengthening the relationship with open, honest communication. Now there are those who will engage in cuckolding, and many men get very worried about this, which is when the queen decides she will be with another man and you as her supportive gentleman will be present or not. This is something to be done right; it must be discussed at length, and both people must approve of it. Any inability to agree on it means it falls into the realm of cheating. In female-led relationships there may be many different things introduced: threesomes, cuckolding, swapping, chastity, discipline, flogging. As long as there is open communication by both you and your queen you are free to engage in any extra activities you feel will enhance your relationship, but never deviate from the core principles that the queen is in charge and you must do everything you can to support her. A female-led woman is the kind of woman who believes that sex is for her pleasure. She believes that men find their purpose and meaning from loving, obeying, and serving women from the boardroom to the bedroom. She believes that women are superior to men but that if a man becomes a gentleman, he can be a valuable asset to her life. She will give a man the respect and love he desires, if he is obedient and serves her well.

If you want to be with a Love & Obey woman, who runs a female-led life, you will absolutely need to become a master at serving your queen in many ways, and oral sex to spice up the bedroom must become the norm. Every sex session must be dedicated to the queen and her needs. Then you may have your needs fulfilled after her. There must be time for open, honest communication about the sex performance so you can improve and become the best lover you can be. You will need to insist on this, as it is something men are not good with. You will take charge of ensuring that the sex remains exciting with the planning of sex escapes and date night. Women love a take-charge man they can rely on to do these things. Love & Obey men are not wimps, weak, and useless. They are successful, confident, supportive gentlemen in service to their queen. When she wakes up, you as her man will begin your day of service for her. Perhaps she wants you to make coffee for her, bring her breakfast, or go down on her for a pleasant morning orgasm or two. She can't wait to get started with her day and tell you what to do. She is the woman who has found and created herself a loving relationship with a man who worships her. You will be totally obedient to her, or at least work on being totally obedient. Your relationship is based on worshipping her, and in return, she respects your gentlemanly skills. There is no equality in this relationship. She is the boss, and he is the worker. She is the general, and you are the soldier. For his service to her, she will give him her love and affection. She will become his passion in life, and he lives to serve her. Loving, obeying, and serving his queen, is the purpose of this Love & Obey gentleman. You are a slave to her love, and you operate as a great team, with her as the captain. You must learn the rules and how to complete all the tasks and responsibilities that she assigns to you. You must read *Real Men Worship Women* and develop the proper mindset to be her ultimate slave.

Your job is to take care of yourself, but you don't need to look perfect to be attractive to Love & Obey women. You always need to be willing to help and serve them and be a good boyfriend/husband/father/and friend. If you take care of yourself and polish yourself up, you can be handsome enough, and if you study and read good books, you can be smart enough to get a Love & Obey woman. You bought this book because you have a desire and you believe this is the right time in your life to make the change to serving women sexually. Perhaps for you, first you need to learn to serve sexually, and then you will finally be able to serve in every part of her life. Are you saying, "Wait a minute, I just wanted to learn how to give good head to a woman so I could be a cool guy and get laid more often"? This is only true if you decide it is true! If you are thinking this way, you are living what I call a self-limiting belief system. On the other hand, some men can be domesticated and live their dream of loving a great and powerful woman. You can have higher aspirations to worship the Feminine Divine and your goddess. Just because other guys seem to be instructing you to still be a womanizer and woman hater, it doesn't mean you need to be one.

As part of your duty as the supportive gentleman, you must take care of your health. Research shows that two in five women are with a man that has erectile dysfunction (ED), and more than 50 percent of men between forty and seventy have ED. This means you will need to invest some time and energy into your health. Eating a proper diet, getting exercise, and managing stress are all great ways to maintain an overall high level of wellness.

CHAPTER 16

Now you have learned the origins of oral sex, how to perform it correctly, and how to create the perfect female-led relationship for you and your queen. Now we will dive into how to deal with introducing oral sex into a new relationship or where it has not been the focus.

Women get a pleasurable feeling of authority, and men get a wonderful feeling of submission when they press their mouths on a delicious pussy. Women also get the opportunity to relax, lie back, and let their fantasies run wild as their man is licking her pleasure palace. But for women who are in the process of growing out of the patriarchal sexual shame that most women grow up with, it can be frightening to have their partner up close and personal with their vagina. For them, the idea of a man down there can bring up negative body images created by misogynist men in their lives who may have shamed them and ignited fears about how their vagina looks, smells, and tastes. Instead of thinking about how many orgasms she is about to have from oral sex, she is worrying about what you are going to think of her pussy. These issues can be very deep-seeded and crippling to a woman's pleasure. This is why I made such a big deal about complimenting your woman's pussy and making her feel like you really love it. You love everything about it: her taste, scent, and appearance. Fortunately, not all women will feel this way, including women who want to live in female-led relationships. But for many women, the intimacy of oral sex and the ability for a woman to demand it and enjoy it will cultivate a beautiful level of communication and tenderness. The intimacy and sexual closeness that oral sex provides is incredibly arousing for female-led couples. When you're with a female-led lover, going down on her will provide a powerful rush of erotic intimacy, and you will find it a very powerful aphrodisiac. Couples in long-term female-led relationships discover that oral sex is a main part of your sex life, creates exciting new channels of erotic play, and deepens intimacy and ignites potent erotic sparks between you both.

But many women have convinced themselves that they don't like oral sex, and often they will try to convince their man of it too. There are also many instances of men wanting to give oral sex, but they do not know how to approach the subject or begin. Previously you may have been unsure of your technique and worried about even doing it for fear of criticism from your goddess. But all of these are just reasons based in insecurity. Once a woman feels comfortable with allowing you to go down on her, everything changes, but the insecurities may take some time to address.

To begin with, research shows that issues over body image for both men and women are growing. When most people think of body image, they think about how attractive they are, physical appearance, how beautiful. But *Psychology Today* suggests that body image is our mental representation of ourselves and it influences behavior, feelings, beliefs, plans, who we choose as a partner, our work, and our day-to-day interactions. So the more that you as the supportive gentleman can influence your queen's outlook and how she perceives herself, the more relaxed and happier she will be.

Women always complain of not feeling like their man really appreciates them or finds them sexy. Women often compare themselves to other women because deep down they consider them to be competition. But what if your queen had you reassuring her daily that she is supreme and that you only care about one thing: bringing her as much pleasure as possible. How would that change things for both of you? How would it transform your relationship?

Research shows that 56 percent of women are unhappy with their overall appearance – their abs and stomach, body weight, hips, and muscle. What was even more shocking was 63 percent of men also had issues with overall appearance, and similar to women, they were unhappy with abs, chest, and muscle. Why is this important? Well, much of our behavior stems from these deep-seated issues with body image. I can recall my own experiences with being overweight and never feeling like I was good enough to be having sex with a man. I can recall wearing heavy shapewear and being very paranoid when it came time for a man to discover what was under all of my clothes. I feel that it was this insecurity that may have driven me to the opposite spectrum of working out until I resembled an Olympic athlete. Similarly, you and your queen may be harboring some of these issues, and it is important to address and overcome them in a positive manner. Serving your queen and accepting everything about her is the first step. Men who are critical immediately put the woman on the defensive, and an unhappy woman means an unhappy life and sex life. A woman is much less likely even to be interested in regular sex much less experimenting with oral sex, different positions, toys, and props. How a woman feels about her body and how she thinks you think about her body will make a huge difference in how relaxed she is during sex, enough to really enjoy it. So your job will entail bolstering her ego and how she feels each and every day. You can tell her how beautiful she is, how much you love her stomach, breasts, thighs. You should be flirty throughout the day, not just during foreplay. Go shopping with her, help her to choose sexy clothing, and be open to when she expresses her insecurities. "Honey, how does my butt look in these jeans?" should be met with, "You're gorgeous," or "You look incredible." Some women may disagree with this approach, but women are suckers for flattery. That said, how you treat your queen should never be fake or false. A smart sophisticated woman will always know if you are lying. *Psychology Today* research reveals that 89 percent of women wanted to lose weight. They also found that more than 57 percent felt inadequate in their twenties, which is when many relationships begin to form. Forty percent of women also indicated that their partner's opinion of their appearance was extremely important to body image.

So chances are your goddess could be unhappy with her body and will need some reassurance from you. Many women indicate that if their partner sees them as beautiful, they are more likely to feel beautiful and rely less on their own criticism. This is an opportunity for you not only to be a great lover, but a great partner. Part of being a great partner is to show unconditional support to your goddess and to accept her for all of her strengths and weaknesses. The more you can do this in daily life, the more it spills over into your sex life. Research shows that twice as many people judge sexual experiences as a source of good feelings rather than bad. For both sexes, interpersonal and emotional factors more often serve to reinforce, not punish. This is encouraging news; it implies that there are many avenues for us to improve our feelings about our bodies. There is no doubt that sexual experiences affect our body image, and our body image affects our sex. The less attractive you or your queen feel, the less likely you are to enjoy the sexual experience and the less relaxed she will feel about opening up to oral sex. This affects you too since 70 percent of men say that sexual experience affects their general life and their self-image. The moral of the story is that there are so many factors which can affect your relationship and your sex life, so open communication is the best way to solve many of the issues which often lead to the negativity which eventually leads to the destruction of relationships.

A popular misconception about oral sex labels one partner as "active" and the other as "passive." In a female-led relationship, men "giving head" and women "getting head" are both actively receiving great pleasure. Men who "give head" deserve respect for their service. In this view, pleasure is received by the woman spreading her legs and the man opening his mouth. Men in female-led relationships do eroticize control issues, and they find giving head really arouses them, and they love it and get great pleasure from giving a woman head. This is what Love & Obey gentlemen are all about. You get genuine, authentic pleasure from giving head to women. You will enjoy performing oral sex for the submissive sensations it gives them, just as much as the woman enjoys receiving it for the powerful dominant sensations it gives her. The truth is, Love & Obey couples are both active and enjoy the dynamic power exchange of men giving and women receiving. Women receiving and men giving is the norm in FLR, and this lifestyle creates unbelievable moments of heart-stopping, naked, and totally exposed intimacy.

Traditional relationships approach oral sex as an added thing to do, a naughty experiment in which both participants are embarking on a pleasure-seeking investigation. In a female-led relationship, it is the opposite. It is the main event, an opportunity to raise the vibration and connect to the spiritual realm. Cunnilingus can be perceived as naughty by patriarchal society, and these old-fashioned male-led couples may experiment to feel wicked about going down on a woman for a few minutes. We see this portrayed in movies. I always find the movie *50 Shades of Grey* interesting. It is promoted to be about BDSM where the man is in control, but watch the finer aspects of the movie, and you will see that the man is actually being controlled. Christian is giving Anna a lot of oral sex pleasure. Anna has the power in both her main relationship and the effects on driving other men crazy. There is only one scene where Christian Grey whips her, and after that she puts a stop to it, essentially changing the relationship to be female-led. I believe that it is those finer points where Christian Grey is satisfying Anna completely and there is much less focus on his own pleasure, though he tries to suggest that his perversion stems from the relationship with his mother. But in true FLR, the women are the power characters in that movie, which means it was much more about female-led relationships. So even the media recognizes that the old is out. Male-dominated, patriarchal, male-led relationships are on the decline with female-led on the rise, which makes it even more important for you to become a master of oral sex. Female leaders demand it, and you will need to give it.

CHAPTER 17

L et's investigate the psychology of why women are still against oral sex and how you can help to change this. When a woman feels confident in her look, taste, and scent down there, she will even enjoy kissing her man after he goes down there. She will enjoy tasting what he just tasted and enjoy sharing the taste on his lips and her lips together after an extra wet oral sex session. When I was working on this book, I discovered that quite a few women were very uncomfortable and got no pleasure from receiving oral sex. They are uptight about it and don't like having their men down there. They don't even understand why a man would like to go down on a woman. If they reluctantly agreed to it, they were simply allowing their boyfriends to do it because they thought they liked it. Even then, they would just lie passively and wait, enduring it with no pleasure until the end. I wondered how they could not realize it was so great. I personally had experienced all of these incredible orgasms from it, and I couldn't imagine living without it.

Most women are lucky enough to orgasm during an initial oral sex experience. These fortunate women experience some early pleasure and learn to improve the experience each time and increase the quality and quantity of their orgasms by naturally testing and trying different techniques and positions until they create their unique style of receiving and orgasming from oral sex. So not only do you as a man need to learn the basic techniques and positions in this book, but you need to pay attention to each individual woman. You have to be sensitive to each woman's style of receiving.

Some women even discover the pleasure of oral sex for the first time with another female during high school or college experimentation with girl-on-girl sex. They may test their lesbian or bisexual tendencies by taking a walk on the wild side with a lesbian friend or a bi-curious college roommate. Most lesbian and bisexual women are more than happy to help a heterosexual woman experiment. Lesbians and bi women are also enthusiastic and excited about an invitation to have sex with another woman, and that enthusiasm is a key turn-on in the oral sex arena. If you do try it, paraphrasing Katy Perry's famous song "I Kissed a Girl," you just might say, "I tried going down on a girl, and I liked it," and after that you will probably love giving it as much as getting it. But if talking your woman into a bisexual experience is a little more than you think she would be willing to do, then you will have to show her that you are eager to please her down there and offer some serious compliments. As I explained earlier in the Oral Sex by Numbers sections of this book. The point of all this is that most women have to learn how orgasm from oral sex; it does not come automatically.

So you must seduce her into it, by being very excited and enthusiastic about going down on her. Once you get down there and give her her first oral orgasm, her opinions about oral sex will quickly change, trust me. The biggest part of this whole problem comes from the media and advertising. Millions of dollars go into douche and tampon commercials in magazines, TV, and online to prove it. Growing up, women are taught our vaginas are nasty, dirty things. It's horrible, but the misogynist, patriarchal-based religions and social teachings of the past few centuries have tried to convince us that the female sex organ is filthy, which we now know is medically false. In fact, a normal healthy vagina is the cleanest place in the body. It's is even cleaner than the mouth. But still, our discomfort remains, and for so many reasons. However, this social conditioning has caused millions of women to have low opinions of their pussies. They think they are smelly and gross. This same social conditioning actually causes many women to have a stigma against lesbians. They think lesbians are gross because they love to put their faces in pussies.

So if your woman is wondering why you want to put your face between her legs and lick, kiss and suck her down there, you need to convince her that her pussy is beautiful, smells great, and tastes delicious, and that it really turns you on to be close to her. Women feel uncomfortable about the way their pussies look, smell, and taste because they have been socially conditioned since they were young that it is dirty down there. It is really tragic that society would promote such a bold-faced lie simply to keep women down and destroy their self-esteem. You can actually be part of the Love & Obey movement, guys. You can start re-conditioning your women that their pussies are in fact BEAUTIFUL! Whether your woman has more, less, or no hair, two big plump outer mounds, a set of uneven inner lips, a big or small clit, or a slit like a dolphin where you can't see any details. You need to tell her you love it! Mother Nature obviously loves pussy and wants women to have all different kinds to celebrate that fact. It's never the same thing twice, no matter how much *Playboy* airbrushes us into sameness. (The vulvas you've seen in men's magazines are airbrushed, waxed, and covered in makeup – some have even had plastic surgery.)

This is your opportunity to join a movement which is fighting back against the misogynist religions and social groups and promote the great things about oral sex.

Encourage your woman to be more open and accepting of her vagina. Men have long been proud of their penises; just look at the number of sculptures and art that proudly display the penis. The David sculpture in Florence is a great example of how the male form was worshipped and depicted. We need more sculptures and paintings of the vagina. We've come a long way, baby, but we still need to go farther.

Today, men are usually allowed more sexual "forgiveness" and are evaluated with more acceptance and even respect as "playboys" relative to their sexual behavior and the number of sexual partners they have. When women engage in the same behavior, with the same number of partners as men, they are considered sluts. In terms of women enjoying and wanting sex and even becoming sexually aggressive, we have reached a historic point in sexual history: a point in time where women are no longer sluts if they like sex. *Slut* is defined disparagingly in the dictionary. A slut is a promiscuous woman: a woman who has many sexual partners. Isn't that what men do? So is a slut a woman with the same morals as a man? There has been such a double standard when it comes to women, men, and sex. Many misogynist men still consider heterosexual sex as something a man does to a woman. For these men, the woman's role is diminished because the focus falls on the pleasure of the man and not that of the woman. When sex is seen as something men are in control of, it is harmful, has negative repercussions on a relationship, and can even ruin both the man's and the woman's sexual health. When men and women are in a traditional male-led sexual relationship, these male-dominated gender roles appear in the bedroom. So when it comes to oral sex, it is understandable that many women are not always ready or comfortable to have oral sex performed on them with the focus on their pleasure. If a woman asks for oral sex or demands to be brought to orgasm orally, she may be viewed as a slut. So many women will voice their discomfort with oral sex performed on them and offer to perform it on you as the man instead. You can change all of this by supporting your queen, mastering oral sex, and promoting the Love & Obey lifestyle. The more men are encouraged to partake and feel comfortable allowing their women to lead, the happier, deeper, and more long-lasting relationships we will create. Each and every day, you will need to bolster your queen's confidence. You will need to put her on a pedestal and reassure her that she is beautiful, all of her, and that you accept her by accepting to serve her completely inside and outside the bedroom. You will listen to her and make her the commander-in-chief in your life, and at no time will you ever show disrespect. You will master the techniques of oral sex and place her needs first, and ensure she is satisfied each and every day, because despite what history tells us, you cannot argue the adage of "happy wife, happy life." The Love & Obey movement is here to stay. Women are growing in their power, and they show no signs of slowing down. You want to learn to service your woman better or find a female-led relationship, you must begin with the basics. You must understand intuitively how to really connect and satisfy a woman sexually through oral sex. Anyone can stick the penis in and have an orgasm, but it takes a real master, a real connoisseur of the art of giving oral sex, to become the most important person in a woman's life. I believe that this is the key to a happy, successful relationship.

CHAPTER 18

I would like the opportunity to now share some real-life examples of how our readers were changed with oral sex and creating a female-led relationship.

Here's what Jason had to say, "When I was younger, there was a married woman who lived next door to me. She was blonde and sexy, and I would talk to her. One day she invited me into her house and sat me down in the living room. She said give me a minute, and she left the room. I was sitting there, trembling with excitement but nervous about what was happening. I heard the shower go on and wondered what she was up to. A few minutes later she called out to me to come into her master bedroom and bathroom. She was standing there, wearing nothing but a white terrycloth towel. She opened it, and she looked like some kind of *Playboy* playmate. She was thirty or older, but her body was lean and beautiful. She told me that I was not going to have sex with her because she was a married woman, but then she said she was going to let me lick her pussy. I was worried at that moment because I had never experienced cunnilingus. I was eighteen years old, and this was the first time I would go down on a woman. She told me that performing oral sex on a woman is a sure-fire way to give her an orgasm, and she was going to tell me what to do.

I'd never seen a pussy that up close and personal before, and as I spread her legs and I gently touched her lips with my fingers, all I could think about was how beautiful she was. I licked her once and immediately knew I'd be begging her to let me do it from then on. Some said this woman was a selfish, rich bitch, but I saw her as a beautiful woman who knew what she wanted. From that moment on I knew the joy of being a "giver." In my opinion, a man may want to perform cunnilingus for many different reasons, but the single most important motivation for going down on a woman should be to give her erotic pleasure. Cunnilingus is a direct way of bringing a woman pleasure, and for me, participating in her pleasure, climaxing a woman, is very arousing – in fact, for me, it's my biggest turn-on. I love making women wet and bringing them to orgasm. Climaxing a woman is a powerful aphrodisiac and the true allure of oral sex for me. Ever since that experience, I am always drawn to go down on women to make them feel good – because a woman's pleasure makes me feel good. There may be other motivating factors involved, but even today, I love to go down on women. The smell, the taste, being up close to a woman's pussy; sometimes it makes me horny just to think about it. I enjoy cunnilingus and definitely get off on knowing how much pleasure I can offer to women. But lately, I have realized that I also enjoy being "used" by women as their boy sex toy. Maybe because of this experience I had as a young eighteen-year-old, but even today one of the best ways for me to get aroused is to go down on a woman. I also love climaxing women with oral sex, the way she taught me to do it so many years ago. She taught me about the tenderness and the spiritual connection of worshiping between the thighs of a beautiful goddess like her. Today, I live in a female-led relationship and follow the Love & Obey movement. I read *Real Men Worship Women* and learned how to live a happy female-led love life. If you are like me, you could be the type of man that savors the feelings, smells, and flavors of an aroused pussy, or you might just enjoy holding the center of your lover's pleasure so intimately in your mouth. For me it takes nothing more than a twinkle in her eye, a smile on her face, or the swish of her hair to spark my desire to kiss and lick my woman's pussy.

This is a testimonial as to how important oral sex is for women in female-led relationships, by, let's call her, Kristin: "When my boyfriend goes down on me, I feel like we're at our closest level of intimacy and that this is something truly special for us both. Honestly, for me, having him going down on me feels more intimate than even having sex with him. Obviously, it just feels really good, but as a strong woman, I like knowing that my man is completely focused on me and my pleasure. The intimacy that going down on a woman affords both partners is tremendous. I say both partners because intimacy and oral sex for me is a two-way street. Both you and your man want to do something that requires a great deal of intimate trust, and both of you may feel like you're running the risk of facing some fear and anxiety. When you're the man who's going down, you may feel insecure about your skills. You have to trust your woman, especially a dominant and demanding woman like me, to withhold criticism and judgment about your ability, performance. But when my man shows a sincere desire to go down on me, I know we can work on those technical issues. I think most of a man's fears about his oral skills and techniques can be managed by simply talking about it together beforehand, during, and after it. For me, sexual communication is huge. Unlike some women who receive oral sex and feel emotionally exposed as well as physically exposed, I am really a confident woman. Personally, I feel empowered when my boyfriend is down between my legs giving me good head. I enjoy oral sex, and I'm proud of that. I discovered my clitoris early on, and when I was younger my lovers seemed to appreciate the fact that I knew where it was. Unlike some women, I definitely do not view oral sex as an appetizer to the main course. For me, I am perfectly happy if oral sex is the only item on the menu, and it offers a wonderful dimension to any sex life. Showing your man how to be a skilled and knowledgeable "downtown" lover and how you like to be tongue licked, lip kissed, mouth nibbled, and sucked is a given for me and something I could never live without."

Some men face a totally different situation than the woman being reluctant to have oral sex. In some cases the man is reluctant to perform oral sex on her. Some men don't like it. These are usually old-school patriarchal or misogynist men who are conditioned by society and their friends to be reluctant about performing oral sex on women. They think that they don't like it. So what happens when one of these men happens to fall for a modern, feminist girl who actually demands that men perform oral sex on her or she'll drop them like a hot plate? What if you are this old-fashioned man in a relationship and a modern woman demands oral sex from you and maybe demands it constantly. What are you supposed to do? How are you supposed to feel about it? Is she normal to demand oral sex? Why is she like this? Shouldn't she just want to do what you, as the man, want to do during sex? Shouldn't she prefer to give you a blowjob?

The belief that women and men are different when it comes to sex and the fact that men and women are held to different standards of sexual conduct is pervasive in contemporary North American society. According to the sexual double standard, teenage boys and men are rewarded and praised for their heterosexual sexual conquests, whereas teenage girls and women are criticized and stigmatized as sluts or whores for similar behaviors.

I will deal with women who don't agree with this social standard. I will deal with women who demand oral sex and explain why that is normal. Researchers at the Kinsey Institute for Research in Sex, Gender, and Reproduction developed a model of human sexual response and provided an organizing explanation that helps our understanding that sex and the desire in women is as strong as the male's sex drive. In truth, it is present and similar in both sexes naturally, and it is conditioned up in men and down in women by patriarchal society and misogynist men.

Researchers looking at sexuality from a scientific perspective understand that men and women are really the same. Now they are figuring out the "why and how" of sexual behavior. These researchers believe that the sexual response mechanism in our brains consists of two universal components: a sexual accelerator and sexual brakes. These components respond to a wide range of different types of sexual stimuli – including genital, visual, and emotional stimulation. A great deal of this emotional stimulation is the result of our upbringing and social conditioning as men and women. So the sensitivity to each stimulus varies from one person to another person. We do know that sexual arousal, desire, and orgasms are universal human experiences, but "why" they happen and "how" we experience them depends largely on the sensitivities of our "brakes" and our "accelerator" and our sensitivity to stimulation, stimulation that is impacted by our social conditioning. This is the basics of the "why and how" of sex. We're all made with sex organs, but in each of us, those organs are organized in a unique way. Our sex organs even go through changes over our lifetimes. Each part of our sexual lifespan can be considered better or worse by us, but in reality, they're just different, and with the right outlook, we can enjoy them all. We all have different desires and needs at different phases in our sex lives. Most people are healthy and normal at the start of our sexual development, and as you grow, if you enjoy the fruits of sex when you begin living a sex life, you continue to have sex with joy in your mind and confidence about your body throughout your life. These fortunate people will grow up as sexually healthy men and women, but even these "healthy" people will be unique in their individual turn-ons and turn-offs. We are all the same sexually in that we are all different sexually. We are all sexually normal in our sexual preferences and differences.

Like all new ways of thinking, female-led relationships have opened up a lot of questions and challenges to much of the preexisting misogynist conditioning and teachings about women and sex. Most men have been told many patriarchal lies about women. In female-led relationships, a power exchange happens between men and women. Women take charge and become the boss in a relationship, sex is now performed for a woman's pleasure, and men view their pleasure as coming from how many orgasms and how much pleasure they can deliver to a woman. The women living this lifestyle are on the edge of a new social revolution where women will become the dominant gender and men will be submissive to women. Obviously this is highly controversial and many men fight this change tooth and nail. But for other men and women who feel broken in the traditional patriarchal sexual roles of society, they realize now with the advent of the Love & Obey movement and the female-led relationship revolution that we've all been lied to, and it is the fault of the misogynist and patriarchal churches and social institutions. Churches and society have done serious damage with their lies. So many women and men come to the Love & Obey movement convinced that they are sexually broken or that there is something wrong with them because they view the roles of men and women differently than they have been taught to view them. They feel dysfunctional, abnormal, anxious, frustrated, and hopeless because they believe that females are superior to men and that females should be relationship and world leaders. That female is the superior gender. They believe women should rule the world. On top of that they believe women should enjoy sex as much as men and that men should serve the needs and desires of women.

Unfortunately, too many social and political leaders, medical professionals, therapists, family members, and boyfriends view this belief in female superiority as sacrilegious and just plain wrong. They believe women are here to love, obey, and serve men and that men are the superior gender. These people believe that women simply don't want sex as much as men. So if you're a woman who does want sex, especially as much as a man, you are immediately called a slut or a whore. I understand the frustration that powerful, sexual alpha women experience, because I am one. Before the Love & Obey movement and the Female-Led Relationship revolution, women like us faced so much frustration and despair, shutting ourselves off from our sexual feelings and desires. We were afraid to express our feminine powers and strong sexuality and demonstrate our mental and emotional superiority. We were caught in a web of misogynist lies, but then we discovered the Female-Led Relationship revolution, and I started this Love & Obey movement. Now this revolution has become our way to get out of the patriarchal trap. Here's what I want you to know right now: women are sexually superior to men once they are freed from their misogynist, patriarchal, and sexual conditioning. So whatever you're experiencing in your sexuality right now with women will change, once you put yourself in a female-led relationship. Yes, your own male sexuality will go on the back burner and you will make her sexual pleasure your number one priority. But I guarantee you that once you help to eliminate your male ego regarding sex and look at the woman as superior, you will discover the amazing world of female-oriented sexual arousal, desire, orgasm, pain, and sensations beyond anything you have ever experienced or even imagined in your life. If you as a man secretly have felt that women are superior to men but you believed that these thoughts and feelings were inappropriate, think again; the patriarchal world is what is inappropriate. You are perfectly normal; it is the outdated patriarchal world around you that's tricked men and women into believing that men are superior, when the opposite is so obviously true. You will see it clearly once you open your eyes. If you want to learn more about this hidden truth, read *Love & Obey*, my book on female superiority. Then read *Real Men Worship Women* and learn the man's true purpose and role in life is to be a gentleman and love, obey, and serve women. That's actually the good news, because now you can open your mind and understand the true roles of men and women, and you can help release your woman's hidden sexual powers, you can begin to take control of your life, and after you read my books, you will reorganize your brain in order to maximize your sexual potential, even in this broken patriarchal world. And when you change your way of thinking, you can change and heal your sexual issues. My books contain information that I have seen transform couples in traditional male-led relationships around the world into female-led relationships. Male-led couples that were unhappy and not experiencing joy in their relationships, today these same couples, and the women in them, are now experiencing sexual well-being because their men are serving the woman's needs. That's why I wrote this book. Men must learn to love and perform oral sex on women as a regular part of their life. I believe it should be done daily, or at least as often as the woman desires it, to support men's submission to their women as their loving female authority.

I've also seen my books transform men's understanding of women, so they

finally see the light and recognize women's natural superiority. I've seen so many male-based relationship couples look at each other and say, "Oh, why didn't we switch years ago!" So many couples have asked me, "Why didn't anyone tell us this before? It explains everything!" I know for sure that female-led relationships are superior and work better than male-led relationships. I know this from my experience and the experience of the hundreds of thousands of couples following me, around the world. Many of these couples write to me on my social media every day, thanking me for speaking the truth. I will tell you to read my books and understand that you are normal if you view women as superior. Everything about female-led relationships is normal. Today, you can start to enjoy the rest of your life with confidence that living in a female-led relationship is normal – now you can experience the joy of living to worship women. Yes, learn the essential skills of giving oral sex to women; it will soon become a way for you to worship your woman. Learn to live to love, obey, and serve your woman as your loving female authority. This is my secret and the secret of hundreds of thousands of couples all around the world discovering real happiness in a female-led relationship.

Yes, people are different and female-led relationships may not be for everyone, but they may be right for you. Letting a woman take control of you, performing oral sex on her may create a spontaneous desire in you to love, obey, and serve her. Showing a woman how much you worship her with oral sex may create a responsive desire in her and allow her to understand that she should be the center of attention and she should be served by a man. She can experience her natural superiority as a woman. Yes, women vary as well. Some women are naturally alpha women, like Jessica, and here is her story:

"My name is Jessica, and I enjoy being a woman and wouldn't ever want to be a man. I like the way my pussy looks and smells. I like to watch myself in the mirror when I masturbate. I enjoy masturbating lying on my back and rubbing my pretty, big clitoris with my hand. Unlike many women, I am proud that I am just as sexual as the men I know. I think I am an alpha woman and perhaps I have more testosterone than most women and maybe even some men. I always knew since I was young that my sexuality is more like a man's sexuality. I love to be sucked and fucked. I know my clitoris is larger than most women's, but I'm not a freak in any way. Most of my friends and men describe me as very feminine and very sexy. However, I know my clit is big. You know those baby carrots they sell at the grocery store? Yes, that's my size. Perhaps it is bigger because I have more testosterone because I have always been athletic and worked out, which in turn made me somewhat muscular and a very horny lady.

"I like masturbating and do it in front of a full-length mirror because I think my pussy is beautiful. I like watching my fingers moving in and around the lips of my pussy. I started when I was a teenager. I was simply curious about what I looked like, so I got a mirror and started checking out my pussy. Obviously, I noticed my clit, but I didn't know until I got older that it was bigger than most. I enjoy masturbating, I enjoy the spray of a shower head on my clit, I enjoy vibrators, and I love my orgasms."

Women like Jessica are like Wonder Woman. They are Amazon goddesses. They are alpha women, but not all women are like that. Some women are very submissive and sexually suppressed. I believe this submissive behavior is much more the result of centuries of being conditioned and programmed down by misogynist churches and social institutions than being a normal state for women. In our society, women are trained to be submissive, even if they feel naturally dominant. Their female power is not released until they are mentally freed from this conditioning to be themselves. So be proud of your woman if she is dominant and wants oral sex. If she wants you to focus on her pleasure, experience her female sexuality, do it with pride. Find purpose in serving your woman's desires and needs. If you are lucky enough to be with a powerful, alpha, and superior woman already, be proud and understand that she is not abnormal. If your alpha woman's sexual desire is incredibly high, be proud of her, don't criticize her.

Early on I noticed there was something important to my social media followers – both men and women – about feeling "normal," and somehow my books have cleared a path to that feeling. The social experience of females leading in relationships and being free to enjoy sexuality is new, and there is much still to be experienced and learned. But this young social experiment has already discovered truths about women as leaders and women's sexuality enough so as to have transformed my followers' relationships with each other and their sex lives, and these truths have certainly transformed mine. I write my books to share the positive stories and sexual insights that prove to us that, despite our misogynist culture's vested interest in making women feel broken, dysfunctional, unlovely, and unlovable, we are in fact fully confident, powerful women who enjoy sex. No matter where you are in your sexual journey, whether you are still in a male-led relationship or you want to expand and experience the awesomeness of a female-led relationship. You can experience a better sex life and you will improve your sex life by adding oral sex for your woman to it. And you'll discover that even if you don't yet feel that way now, once you open your mind and experience a female-led relationship, you will never go back to the old way.

www.ingramcontent.com/pod-product-compliance
Lightning Source LLC
Chambersburg PA
CBHW021238090426
42740CB00006B/590